"This book is urgently neede don't help their members or l̲.... Christians not to be afraid of their own deaths. His numerous ideas also teach us how to accompany other people to their deaths. I pray this book will enable many congregations to develop new practices and programs for the elderly and their caretakers."

MARVA J. DAWN, author of *Being Well When We're Ill, My Soul Waits* and *In the Beginning, GOD*

"Every seminarian and parish minister should read this book. Rob Moll recovers the Christian tradition's lost teaching on preparing for death. He then offers theologically sound guidance for families and clergy as they serve the dying and then honor their legacy. Indispensable."

DAVID NEFF, editor in chief and vice president, Christianity Today Media Group

"Dying has for many today, like sex in the nineteenth century, become the great unmentionable. But this brave, realistic, well-researched and well-digested book restores the 'good death,' as the climax of faithful discipleship, to the Christian radar screen. On going home to God, and helping others on the same journey, what is said here is excellent from every point of view."

J. I. PACKER, professor of theology, Regent College, and author of *Knowing God*

"*The Art of Dying* takes the fear out of dying and replaces it with rich models of dying well. Drawn from a broad spectrum of historical, theological, bioethical, social and practical resources, interlaced with captivating narrative, *The Art of Dying* paints a vision of what dying and grieving with the Christian community has looked like—and once again should look like. While it is particularly relevant for every Christian who will die, other mortals will benefit from reading over our shoulders."

PAIGE COMSTOCK CUNNINGHAM, J.D., executive director, The Center for Bioethics & Human Dignity

THE ART OF DYING

LIVING FULLY INTO THE LIFE TO COME

ROB MOLL

FOREWORD BY LAUREN WINNER

IVP Books

An imprint of InterVarsity Press
Downers Grove, Illinois

InterVarsity Press
P.O. Box 1400, Downers Grove, IL 60515-1426
World Wide Web: www.ivpress.com
E-mail: email@ivpress.com

InterVarsity Press® is the book-publishing division of InterVarsity Christian Fellowship/USA®, a movement of students and faculty active on campus at hundreds of universities, colleges and schools of nursing in the United States of America, and a member movement of the International Fellowship of Evangelical Students. For information about local and regional activities, write Public Relations Dept., InterVarsity Christian Fellowship/USA, 6400 Schroeder Rd., P.O. Box 7895, Madison, WI 53707-7895, or visit the IVCF website at <www.intervarsity.org>.

All Scripture quotations, unless otherwise indicated, are taken from the Holy Bible, New International Version®. NIV®. Copyright 1973, 1978, 1984 by International Bible Society. Used by permission of Zondervan Publishing House. All rights reserved.

While all the stories in this book are true, in some instances, names have been changed to protect the privacy of those involved.

Design: Cindy Kiple
Cover image: Nacivet/Getty Images
Interior image: iStockphoto

ISBN 978-0-8308-3736-6

Printed in the United States of America ∞

Library of Congress Cataloging-in-Publication Data

Moll, Rob, 1977-
   The art of dying: living fully into the life to come / Rob Moll.
      p. cm.
   Includes bibliographical references (p.   ).
   ISBN 978-0-8308-3736-6 (pbk.: alk. paper)
   1. Death—Religious aspects—Christianity. I. Title.
BT825.M55 2010
236'.1—dc22
                                                                    2010000188

| **P** | 18 | 17 | 16 | 15 | 14 | 13 | 12 | 11 | 10 | 9 | 8 | 7 | 6 | 5 | 4 | 3 | 2 | 1 |
| **Y** | 25 | 24 | 23 | 22 | 21 | 20 | 19 | 18 | 17 | 16 | 15 | 14 | 13 | 12 | 11 | 10 |

To Clarissa and the kids,

Fiona, Colin, and Christian

CONTENTS

FOREWORD

O~N A BOOKCASE IN MY OFFICE,~ I have a cup full of nineteenth-century rings: some feature skeletons, some hold locks of hair. These were mourning rings—rings that people wore in memory of dead parents, spouses, friends. The rings are engraved with the decedent's initials, and sometimes with a death date. This was a commonplace practice in the eighteenth and nineteenth century, this exchanging of mourning rings. The rings helped the bereaved continue to feel close to their dead. And the rings kept the reality of death ever before people, intimately wrapped around their fingers.

Americans have largely given up mourning jewelry. Indeed, we have given up a whole host of embodied and communal practices of death that once shaped how Americans died and grieved.

If you had been, say, a middle-class white woman in the United States 175 years ago, an elaborate choreography of death and mourning would have been familiar to you. You would have passed countless hours at the deathbeds of friends and relatives who died at home. There, one of your tasks would have been to help the dying person realize that she was in fact dying. You were

there, in part, to encourage your friend to make her peace with
friends, relatives and God. You would have visited homes of bereaved neighbors and encountered corpses, laid out awaiting
burial, in their parlors. You would have regularly walked among
tombstones—in your churchyard, or perhaps even in your back-
yard. You would have been accustomed to meeting men and
women in mourning garb—black armbands for men, dresses
made of drab black fabric for women. Their mourning clothing
would have told you, wordlessly, of their grief. You would probably have worn mourning clothing yourself at some point. Your
bombazine or crepe gown would have helped you live into your
mourning—and the social convention telling you when to put
the black dress away would have given you an important calen-
dar, telling you when mourning was to end, telling you when to
resume the rhythms of life fully among the living.

For Christians in most times and places, death has been a routine part of life. But during the last century, Americans have
embraced an unprecedented denial of death, an unprecedented
evasion of death. In general, we have removed death from our
homes. People no longer die there; corpses no longer repose
there before burial. We no longer allow people to say that they
are dying—rather, they are "battling" an illness. Far from encouraging the perilously ill to recognize the imminence of their
death, we encourage the sick (and their doctors) to fight death—
but not to prepare for it. Most of us live far from graveyards,
which we now locate on the periphery of suburbs, not in our
backyards, not in places we routinely encounter. And rather than
acknowledge the long unfolding of mourning, we praise bereaved people for the speed with which they get back to normal
after their husband or mother or friend dies.

Some would say this evasion of death is an improvement. Some would say my mourning rings are macabre. I would say our avoidance of death, far from being an advance, is false, costly and alienating. We, the church, need to recover the art of dying. We need to reacquaint ourselves with death. We need to help people die well and mourn well. We need to lament. We need to allow dying Christians to be just that—dying Christians, who can rail against, but also prepare for, death. We need to make space for the exhausting, sad work of mourning.

The history of dying that Rob Moll sketches here, and the practices of dying and mourning well that he describes, illustrate the rich resources we have for a recovered, reimagined art of dying. I hope that people will read this book—and talk about it, and take inspiration from it. I hope we will let Rob Moll's insights help us become communities where people can reckon with, rather than dodge, death.

Lauren Winner
Assistant Professor of Christian Spirituality
Duke Divinity School

1

WHEN DEATH ARRIVES

Our culture simply doesn't know what to think about death. Through medicine and science we know more about death and how to forestall it than ever before. Yet we know very little about caring for a dying person. We don't know what to expect or how to prepare for our own death. And we're often awkward at best when trying to comfort a friend in grief.

Our culture is fighting, and sometimes succeeding, to expand the so-called right to die. We hear stories of the compassion of family members and doctors who assist in the deaths of terminally ill patients. Yet our doctors and hospitals are astounding in their ability and passionate desire to rescue cancer sufferers, accident victims or heart-attack patients. We have come to expect medical breakthroughs, vaccines and wonder-working drugs.

There is no shortage of books, studies and experts ready to explain our culture's fear of death or our eagerness to avoid it. Yet some of our bestsellers—*Tuesdays with Morrie, The Last Lecture, 90 Minutes in Heaven*—feature stories about people dying, or nearly so, and the lessons they discovered at the end of life. Celebrities give a whole society the opportunity to follow along in the struggle with a terminal disease and publicly, at least on TV, mourn their deaths.

Having volunteered with hospice patients and worked with grieving families at a funeral home, I've seen the results of this confusion firsthand. Interviewing families, doctors and hospice workers, it's clear that our paradoxical approach to death is largely due to the fact that we are strangers to death—despite it being ever present. Caring for elderly parents is typically our first prolonged and engaged confrontation with death. Even then, however, doctors and nurses often guide us through the experience. It's not unusual for children to care for their parents from a distance, calling doctors or arranging transportation and nursing care, further removing us from face-to-face interaction with death and dying.

Death is all around us, however. Our movies are filled with violent deaths. Daily news reports feature wars that may involve our own neighbors, family members or church friends. We receive appeals from development agencies and news outlets to help ethnic groups, such as those in Darfur, targeted for violence by more powerful neighbors. We are asked to support relief workers caring for people struck by famine, natural disasters or epidemics.

I remember my first experience, after college, in a group that met weekly for prayer. I was amazed that, unlike my college experiences praying with friends, more than half of our prayer requests were for health issues. Often we prayed for people with potentially life-threatening illnesses. Some acquaintances at work went on leave as they received chemotherapy, and some of them never recovered. Often we prayed, as colleagues awaited test results, "Lord, let it turn out to be nothing at all."

Even at a young age, we are around death. A friend from my

high school youth group killed herself. Another friend from college died one summer in a car accident. My brother's youth group volunteer was murdered at a highway rest stop. Facebook friends fill their updates with information on ailing relatives.

Tragic as these incidents are, however, they are not the same as a sustained face-to-face encounter with a loved one on his deathbed. They don't affect our lives in the same way. Prayer requests and Facebook updates do not breed familiarity. While they can and should lead us to reflect on our own death and encourage us to live in the light of our mortality, often our busy lives don't allow this reflection. Death, while ever present, is ever more removed from our firsthand experience.

The average American's first intimate encounter with death might not occur until she is well beyond middle age. "Until their loved ones lie in the last light," author Stephen Kiernan says, "families today do not know mortality."[1] In fact, as people routinely live into their nineties, it is now not unusual to have elderly children taking care of their even more elderly parents.

When we are finally called on to be with a dying loved one, we must learn what to do and how to behave on the fly. This is a drastic change from the days when dying was a more familiar, if an equally unwelcome, presence. "All the things that once prepared us for death," writes journalist Virginia Morris, "regular experience with illness and death, public grief and mourning, a culture and philosophy of death, interaction with the elderly, as well as the visibility of our own aging—are virtually gone from our lives."[2]

For most of the last century, death has moved steadily away from view. Over the course of the first half of the twentieth century, the site of death moved from the home to the hospital. In 1908, 14 percent of all deaths occurred in an institutional setting, either a hospital, nursing home or other facility. Just six years later the figure had jumped to 25 percent.[3] By the end of the century it was nearly 80 percent.[4]

As the place of death moved to the hospital, people became less familiar with the sights and sounds of the very ill. Medical personnel took over the intimate care of the patient, often simply because their expertise was required. These changes allowed patients to survive—at least temporarily—diseases that would have killed them. But through those exchanges, we forgot what death looks like, and we lost something. We now keep death at a distance. The dying, says historian Phillipe Aries, are pushed out of sight because society cannot endure their presence. While it was once common for friends, family and even strangers to pay respects to someone on her deathbed, Aries says,

> It is no longer acceptable for strangers to come into a room that smells of urine, sweat, and gangrene, and where the sheets are soiled. Access to this room must be forbidden, except to a few intimates capable of overcoming their disgust, or to those indispensable persons who provide certain services.[5]

We have forgotten how to behave as caregivers or simply family and friends. We act clumsily and awkwardly around the grieving, often complicating their mourning. We're clueless about what to say to a person on his deathbed. We ourselves are left feeling confused and uncertain about death's meaning and its affect on our faith and our lives.

But our behavior, it turns out, is rather common and understandable, if still inappropriate to the occasion. "Nowadays, very few of us actually witness the deaths of those we love," writes surgeon and author Sherwin Nuland. "Not many people die at home anymore, and those who do are usually the victims of drawn-out diseases or chronic degenerative conditions in which drugging and narcosis effectively hide the biological events that are occurring."[6] In other words, even those few who have first-hand experience being with someone dying do not fully experience the event—at least not in the way every other society and every other generation throughout history would have.

Living far from our elderly loved ones also removes us from their declining years as well as from their medical care. Adult children find themselves on conference calls with their parents' doctors. They fret about their loved ones' safety when their home is no longer a safe place to live or when driving becomes dangerous. They fly a thousand miles for a surgery, never quite knowing what is happening and if this trip will be the last. And, in interview after interview, I've learned that relatives who live far away have a much stronger tendency to advocate for aggressive therapy, prompting family conflicts when other members, including the dying person, are opposed.

Not only can our unfamiliarity with death make us incompetent when visiting socially with the ill or grieving, we may also make decisions opposed to the best interests of the people we love. A doctor told me recently of a patient who had lived well for two years after deciding to discontinue her chemotherapy treatment.[7] For much of those two years, this woman enjoyed life. She was able to garden, take walks, spend time with her husband and accomplish some final goals she had set for herself. Her mental powers had declined, however. She regularly offered the same joke to her doctor. "Old age is not for cowards," she chuckled, each time thinking it was an original thought.

But eventually she began doing much worse. She was bleeding extensively, and the doctor could not determine where she was bleeding from. Her short-term memory was failing, and she no longer wanted to eat, as happens to dying people.

"What do we do?" the doctor said to me the day after discussing the issue with the woman's husband.

> Do we say, "We're not quite sure what the bleeding is from, but we know she's got lung cancer. We know she's going to die from the lung cancer. She's comfortable. She's weak, but she's not in pain. She's breathing okay, and she's quite content." Do we put her in the hospital, transfuse her, see if this is correctable, and then let her die of the lung cancer, which could be a much more painful death than what she's experiencing now?

She had already lived more than eighteen months longer than she was told she would after refusing chemotherapy.

It is a complicated issue, even for a doctor accustomed to dealing with it. But invariably, the decision becomes more complex once out-of-state relatives are involved. The doctor continued,

> Rarely do I have any dissension when am I talking to people. The dissension comes from those who weren't there. I fully expect when I get to the office this afternoon to have a phone call from the daughter saying, "Why aren't you doing this? Why aren't you doing that?" And I have to go through the whole discussion all over again. Then it will be the son from Arizona.

Confronted by these challenges, we aren't always able to cope. Sherwin Nuland recounts an Alzheimer's patient who had moved from New York to Florida for his retirement. When he was diagnosed with the disease, all his children were still in New York. His wife spent every day with him in the nursing home, and she lovingly cared for him during the remaining years of his life. But his children only visited once. Rather than watching a slow decline, the man's out-of-state children saw one massive drop in their father's health. Horrified, they never visited him again.[8] Their mother supported her children's decision, saying she didn't want them to remember their father this way. This extreme instance illustrates a more general truth: unfamiliarity with death can discourage us from fulfilling our familial responsibilities.

A hospice social worker from the Chicago suburbs told me that the most difficult part of his job is finding people to care for his hospice patients. Typically, they don't require twenty-four-hour nursing care. But often dying people need help using the bathroom, cooking and eating or keeping clean. For many patients, he said, finding someone willing and able to help is nearly impossible.

Though it was a problem in the affluent Chicago suburbs, it was no trouble to find caregivers among the poor communities of Miami, where he used to work. My friend said many impoverished families didn't have material things, but when a loved one was dying, they would drop everything to care for that person. "They knew what was important," he says. These families were much better at caring for their families. Still, such devotion is no longer the norm.

ETHICS VERSUS VALUES

I began writing this book at a time when end-of-life ethics was being hotly debated in the press. Not long before, the doctors for Terri Schiavo, a woman who had been in a persistent vegetative state for roughly fifteen years, had been ordered by a judge to remove a feeding tube and other medical treatment that had been keeping her alive. Her husband and her family had spent years in court trying to gain, or to prevent, such a decision from a judge. Congress became involved and tried to intervene.

While the legal process and the decision reached caused great commotion among the Christian community, as well as the rest of the country, I found few satisfactory answers to the dilemma. While most pastors, theologians and ethicists agreed that it was permissible to withdraw medical treatment, Schiavo's dilemma was more difficult. She only needed food, water and minimal care. Yet her food and water, delivered through a feeding tube, required medical professionals to perform the delicate maneuver to insert the tube. The contents of her food were scientifically and medically determined. She wasn't simply fed pureed pork chops. Even if Schiavo was so ill that removing a feeding tube was ethically defensible, Christians were rightly furious that anyone would be left alone, without care and human comfort, to die. Yet in my own conversations with doctors, theologians and church leaders, they suggested privately that they would never want to be kept alive artificially (even with just food and water) for fifteen years.

I was unsatisfied with Christian responses that either required the prolonging of life—no matter the physical, mental, relational or financial suffering involved—or that pinpointed what treatments might be appropriate under what circumstances. Instead, I wanted to find a Christian response to these issues that would be useful under any medical circumstance, that upheld the value of life and the dignity of the person.

What I discovered was the Christian tradition of the good death. While the particulars of medical technology in the twenty-first century are unique, every age has challenged Christians with difficult questions of how to die well. And every age, including our own, has wrestled with how to teach fellow Christians the meaning of death and the ways they could practice it faithfully. Each age recognized that how a culture approaches death precisely reflects what it believes and how it approaches life. While this is true for any culture, Christians must also reconcile their approach to death with Jesus, the Son of God, whose death and resurrection provides a very specific example of how to die and offers the hope to all Christians of a bodily resurrection in the last day. If we Christians really do enjoy the life of God, who is victorious over death, our life on earth is therefore cast in a very different light.

Century after century Christians rehearsed and applied their beliefs about death; throughout their lives they envisioned dying so that at the moment of death they would be prepared. They sought to die reconciled to God and their human brothers and sisters. They gave evidence of their faith in the life to come, either by professing it or by describing their deathbed visions of the heavenly places, often both. They offered comfort to surviving loved ones who desired to hear the last words of the dying who were so close to the eternal enjoyment of life with God.

Death, Christians believed, was not just a medical battle to be fought, though they did use medicine for healing. Nor was death simply about the loss of precious relationships to be mourned. Instead, this was a spiritual event that required preparation. The dying performed it in public as evidence of their faith and to provide instruction to others. Rather than waiting for illness to overtake them, these Christians were actively involved in their own dying, in control—to the extent possible—of the dying process. Injured at the death of a fellow Christian, the church community then rallied together to grieve and to express once again their faith and knit themselves together in a new way.

As dying in the late twentieth century became a drawn out

process, I also discovered an immense opportunity to relearn and reteach these values. While the question of when or whether to withdraw a feeding tube is still difficult to answer, there are at least certain values we can apply. As we assist others through the process of treating a terminal illness or as we contemplate our own answers to such questions, we can seek to perform these elements of the good death. Whatever the medical decisions made, under any circumstances we can express our faith in God, our love for one another, our hope in the resurrection. Having done this, we will have been faithful, in the eyes of fellow believers throughout history, to God and our neighbor. In the culmination of our lives, we will have said and done what was most important.

AUNT EILEEN

My own first personal encounter with death came when I was twenty-seven years old. My wife and I went to visit my great aunt who was dying of cancer.

My aunt lived alone after her sister died fifteen years earlier. Aunt Eileen lived on the fifth floor of an apartment building on the 1300 block of north Lake Shore Drive. I remembered as a child staring through her window at the city below. Now, as I looked out her window, I thought about those visits when her apartment seemed as if it were set in the clouds. Neither Aunt Eileen nor her sister married. Their nieces and nephews, and their children, were her only family nearby. She lived by herself, but she wouldn't die that way. A few family members, particularly my mom, began regularly visiting her.

For years Aunt Eileen kept her cancer a secret. Even as she neared her eighties, she told no one about her trips across the park that straddled the distance between her apartment building and the hospital, just a few miles north of Chicago's Loop. She walked, not wanting to spend the money on a taxi or ask a family member for a lift to the hospital for chemotherapy. I had visited Eileen seldom in the years before she died. When she'd been sick, she didn't allow visitors. On her deathbed, however, she changed her mind.

I only learned of her illness around the time Eileen entered hospice a few months before her death. Her doctor had urged her to undergo more treatments, but she declined. Having seen hospice at work when her sister died of breast cancer, Eileen preferred to die at home in peace. My mother, who had taken over much of her care, began making dozens of trips to North Lake Shore Drive.

I had made no effort to see her until my mother encouraged me to visit Aunt Eileen. I assumed there was nothing I could do for her, and it never occurred to me to simply drop by to see my dying aunt. When we entered her apartment, the hospice nurse directed us into her bedroom. My aunt lay on the hospital bed brought in by hospice. The only other object in the room was a dresser, and on it stood a mirror. Into the frame, my aunt inserted pictures of saints, Jesus, Mary and Pope John Paul II. A devout Catholic, Aunt Eileen was calling on her spiritual resources as she lay dying in the same one-bedroom apartment she had lived in for decades.

I tried talking to Aunt Eileen, but her speech was slurred and sometimes inaudible. She moaned and attempted to respond to my small talk. Curled on the bed, as if withdrawing into herself, she tugged at the clothes that lay loosely across her body, while the hospice nurse tried to maintain my aunt's modesty. The hospital gown she wore had the back cut off, apparently because the clothes at which she constantly pulled were irritating. She was covered by the partial gown and her sheets, with her knees curled up toward her chest. She would die in only a week, and yet I was eager to get out of this room. My mind raced as I tried to think of something to say.

My wife is an easier conversationalist. She told Aunt Eileen about the recent snowfall. "But I'm used to it," she said while my aunt mustered an inaudible reply, "I grew up in New Hampshire."

I looked around her bedroom and wondered what to do. I'd never tried to make conversation with a dying person. The chit-chat I usually engaged in with my aunt seemed inappropriate, but other topics (How are you feeling?) seemed uncomfortably loaded with the suggestion of her death.

It was the second time my wife and I had visited my aunt since she entered hospice, and each time I stood uncomfortably, said little, and left as soon as I felt it appropriate. I felt awful for Aunt Eileen. I was afraid of this disease that had shriveled her up and left her twisted on the hospital bed in her apartment. I was, to some degree and to my shame, repulsed by my aunt's shrunken figure on that bed. Yet I'd never talked to a dying person before. I had no experience comforting, and certainly not ministering to, people on their deathbeds.

On this final visit, I fell into old routes of conversation. My wife and I talked of old show tunes and movie stars—Fred Astaire and Ginger Rogers. We reminisced about Aunt Eileen's days as a dance instructor, decades before I was born. We read the psalms, yet nothing we could do or say measured up to the gravity of the situation. Eventually, we left, saddened by her impending death, yet feeling helpless to provide her any comfort.

Aunt Eileen died the following week. In some ways her death was good. She gave a few final requests to my mother—instructions for her memorial service (she wanted no funeral) and requests for her favorite food, Dove ice cream bars. And my mom saw that they were completed. Our family visited, and though she was alone during much of her final years, she was not entirely alone at the end. She had her church and the hospice chaplain to care for her spiritually. Her death was good also because it was a mercy, a farewell to the affliction visited upon her. Eileen's sickness had been a great evil. She suffered badly and over a long period.

I believe that Aunt Eileen appreciated our visit, so it had done some good. Yet I felt inadequate to the moment. It was an important event, but I talked about the weather and Ginger Rogers and waited for the first opportunity to leave. I felt that I'd failed in what seemed like a basic responsibility, to comfort a dying family member. Still, I didn't know what I'd done wrong or could have offered or said instead. I, like most Americans, grew up knowing nothing about the end of life. I never watched death's slow advance, as someone gradually loses the ability to drive, to clean windows and then to cook dinner or use the bathroom. I never saw someone's grip on life weaken, and his hopes turn away from this life as he faced the next.

Given the sacredness of such an event, I felt the need to offer more to assist my aunt. How should I care for a loved one on her deathbed? What do you say when no words can be sufficient? I had no idea.

I was bothered by these thoughts long after her memorial. I knew as I grew older these were skills I would need again. But I also realized that I had given almost no thought to this most essential truth of life: I will one day die. What should I think of that, and how should I prepare myself? And how could I help someone near death if I haven't spent time considering my own mortality?

EVIL AND DEATH

While dying well is often a matter of living well, to live well we must come to grips with our death. It is difficult, but it can also be invigorating. "It is only by facing and accepting the reality of my coming death that I can become authentically alive," says the Orthodox bishop Kallistos Ware.

We avoid death or even fear it because death is an evil, the horrible rending of a person from her body, from loved ones, from the ability to be fully in God's image. "Death is not part of God's primary purpose for his creation," writes Ware. "He created us, not in order that we should die, but in order that we should live."[9] Jesus wept at Lazarus's death. The apostle Paul called death the last enemy. Death is indeed evil.

Yet death is also a mercy; it is the final affliction of life's miseries. It is the entrance to life with God. Life's passing can be a beautiful gift of God. This riddle of death's evil and its blessing is not difficult to solve. We enact it every Good Friday as we recall the evil of Christ's death to be followed on Easter Sunday with the joy of his resurrection. We do not rejoice in Christ's death or Judas's betrayal. Yet there is no evil so great that God cannot bring joy and goodness from it. That is why death deserves our attention in life. Because we instinctively want to avoid it, to turn our face away, it is good to look death in the eye and constantly remind ourselves that our hope is in God, who defeated death.

Meditating on one's death has been practiced throughout Christian history. St. Isaac the Syrian instructed,

> Prepare your heart for your departure. If you are wise, you will expect it every hour. . . . And when the time of departure comes, go joyfully to meet it, saying, "come in peace. I knew you would come, and I have not neglected anything that could help me on the journey."[10]

2

GRADUAL DYING AND END-OF-LIFE CARE

W<small>HILE TWENTIETH-CENTURY MEDICINE</small> drastically changed how we die, it has also had a more subtle—but no less profound—effect. Because of modern medicine, dying often takes a long time. One study found that most elderly are diagnosed as having a disease three years before it will eventually end their lives. On top of that a Rand study found that "Americans will usually spend two or more of their final years disabled enough to need someone else to help with routine activities of daily living because of chronic illness."[1] Long before we are visiting loved ones on their deathbed, we may be helping them cook, clean and use the bathroom.

While the period may average three years, many people—particularly women—will spend more than a decade caring for older parents and in-laws. In the coming years, "family care giving—[for so] long the backbone of long-term care—will be heavily burdened," the Rand study predicted. Today's family structures—smaller, often spread across the country and more independent—make it even more difficult to care for the elderly and dying. "Longer durations of illness and greater numbers of women working outside the home also place greater burdens on the pool of potential caregivers."[2]

While the first half of the twentieth century saw the major causes of death change from quick-killing infectious diseases to quick-killing heart diseases or cancer, the end of the century saw those diseases replaced by chronic ones that killed gradually. In 1976 the leading cause of death was heart disease, which typically manifested itself as a heart attack. Strokes were another instant killer. Today, a life-ending heart attack happens at a rate 61 percent below that of thirty years ago. Stephen Kiernan writes that even the death rate from accidents, either on the road or elsewhere, has dropped 36 percent.[3] Rapid response teams are so proficient that they have been able to significantly reduce the number of deaths that occur from such emergencies as car accidents and heart attacks.

Having largely succeeded in treating these, our leading causes of death now advance slowly. Kiernan writes,

> In a recent fifteen-year span, deaths from chronic respiratory disease increased 77 percent. Fatalities from Alzheimer's disease have doubled since 1980. . . . People now succumb to congestive heart failure, lung disease, diabetes that leads to kidney failure, ALS (or Lou Gehrig's disease), Parkinson's, [and] osteoporosis.[4]

Despite the health care system's best efforts and unparalleled success, it has only delayed the inevitable.

A Unique Opportunity

And unfortunately today, fewer people are caring for more elderly.

Chronic illnesses mean that dying takes a longer period of time and involves more complicated medical issues. Despite these challenges, the trend toward gradual dying offers a unique opportunity. "For the first time in human history," Kiernan writes, "we can anticipate our mortality."[5] Of course, the fact of death is not new, but our ability to be reasonably certain that it is or is not around the corner is exceptional. Not only can we look our own death in the eye, but we may have years to do so, during which time we can still work, enjoy family or go on a mission trip. Many Christians find in these final years the opportunity to experience the most valuable years of life.

One gerontologist in the Chicago suburbs confirms the findings of numerous studies. "Less than ten percent of my patients experience unexpected, sudden death," says John Dunlop. He is aware that the thought of a slow decline is frightening to many. "You ask anybody how they want to die today, and they say 'Make it quick,'" he says.

Instead of fearing the slow decline, Dunlop, who has cared for hundreds of elderly patients, says, "I hope I die slowly." A slow death offers opportunities to spend time with family, say goodbye and slowly orient a person toward life with God, he says. "I think most people who have thought it through will say there are more advantages to my family with my dying slow. It's kind of selfish to want to die fast."

Of course, as Christians, we try to spend our entire lives living in view of eternity, not just our final years. But even with the benefit of a lifetime's reflection on our destiny to worship God in his presence, the prospect of imminent death will surely focus our thoughts in new ways. The experience of dying will change us. A slow death also allows modern Christians the opportunity to relearn what it means to die faithfully. Christians have long intentionally practiced their dying to express the belief that we bear the image of God, that Jesus came to earth and died, that Jesus rose from the grave, and so will all those who hope in him.

MIRACLE MAKERS

Despite the opportunities of gradual dying, some Christian thinkers and theologians have tended to focus on the challenging questions of bioethics—how and when to apply or withdraw medical technology. At the same time, individual Christians have often placed their hope in the effectiveness of medical therapies to delay death.

Gradual dying means we must be ever wiser regarding our use of medical treatments, particularly when these interventions are designed to treat sudden emergencies such as car accidents and heart attacks, not necessarily diseases of old age. While CPR, ventilators or radical surgery may be appropriate for an otherwise healthy fifty-year-old man who happens to have clogged arteries, the procedures may not be wise on a frail eighty-five-year-old.

Or they might be. The use of medicine to cure or slow the advance of a disease can be a compelling and effective option amid the uncertainty of an elderly person's long decline.

That is why we must be careful not to place our hope in medicine's ability to provide healing. Its successes can be deceptive. Richard Wunderink, an ICU physician at Northwestern Memorial Hospital in Chicago, told me the families of his patients can't believe it when the medical system is sometimes unable to keep somebody alive. "People are shocked if we can't pull people out [of a life-threatening illness] in an almost Star Wars kind of way," he says. "They think that anything is possible. Families ask for brain transplants and stem cell transplants and regenerative kinds of things."

Our hope in medicine can lead to an unrealistic expectation that medicine can cure whatever disease we or our loved ones might have. Such expectations tempt us to believe we need not contemplate and prepare for our death or that of our family members. "Too often," complains Nuland, "patients and their families cherish expectations that cannot be met, with the result that death is made all the more difficult by frustration and disappointment with the performance of a medical community that may be able to do no better."[6]

Our culture's glorification of youth adds to the difficulties. Companies advertise vitamin supplements or drugs promising cures to any and every ailment. "We have become so fixated on life-prolonging habits," says journalist Virginia Morris, "and so strident in our desire for—indeed, our right to—self-determination, that we have gained a false sense of control over death."[7] We expect that a visit to the hospital, a new pill, an experimental therapy or enough fish oil and Vitamin D will always be able to make us healthy again.

More sadly, Christians often do not offer sympathetic understanding to those dealing with their own or a loved one's illness. Instead, like a pill from the drugstore, some Christians chide the ill with admonishments to have more faith. As though a dose more will tip the scales in their favor.

Yet our natural fear of death can be a hard thing to face. Even though we must know we're deceiving ourselves, the shock of our mortality is too much. Instead we hope for a miracle from God, the pharmaceutical companies or our doctors. And we leave off for another day preparing to die or helping another who is near death. In this way, we often fail to take advantage of the opportunities of gradual dying.

TOO PRO-LIFE?

A study published in the *Journal of the American Medical Association* found that people of religious faith (95 percent of whom were Christians)[8] were three times more likely to choose aggressive medical treatment at the end of their lives, even though they knew they were dying and that the treatments were unlikely to lengthen their lives. The study determined "that relying upon religion to cope with terminal cancer may contribute to receiving aggressive medical care near death."[9] One of the researchers told me, "patients who received outside clergy visits had worse quality of death scores in comparison to those who did not." In other words, our churches are not teaching us to die well. Why?

Those who intensively rely on their faith when suffering from terminal illness, the study found, "may choose aggressive therapies because they believe that God could use the therapy to provide divine healing, or they hope for a miraculous cure while intensive medical care prolongs life." God, however, doesn't need the surgeon's assistance to restore health. Not only did they choose more aggressive medical interventions, the study found religious people were less likely to have done any end-of-life planning or to understand the legal documents involved.

The researchers report that there may be good reasons to pursue aggressive end-of-life care. Many Christians believe it is simply morally wrong to forgo any potential opportunity to increase their life, even if only by a few days. However, as the study notes, "Because aggressive end-of-life cancer care has been associated with poor quality of death and caregiver bereavement adjustment, intensive end-of-life care might represent a negative outcome." One researcher said, "We believe that the problem is that religious people who are dying . . . along with their families are not receiving spiritual counsel in their medical decision making." The researchers say these patients are "not being counseled in how to die."[10]

Aside from increased pain, less ability to interact with family members and other personal challenges, there are also spiritually "negative outcomes." Every Christian doctor, ethicist, pastor or theologian I spoke to believed that while aggressive care had its place, there must come a point when Christians shift their focus from extending life to preparing to die.

For evangelical Christians, making wise decisions at the end of life is complicated by our pro-life commitments. For example, I visited a church in Minneapolis that was holding a conference on end-of-life issues, one of a very few churches that was bringing Christian experts from around the country to discuss the topic. As I walked into the foyer, I saw several displays from organizations and was pleased that so many Christian groups were working on this issue. However, as I got closer I was surprised to see that the only presenters were pro-life groups. Of the many Christian hospice organizations and nursing and medical associations in the country, none were at this conference. No Christian nursing homes, hospitals or retirement communities were there. Only groups interested in preserving the sanctity of life at its beginning. "We're so pro-life," says one Christian gerontologist, "we're anti-death."

Life is equally sacred at its end as at its beginning, of course. And the devaluing of life is equally abhorrent, whether for the convenience of a pregnant woman or the financial interests of an insurance company that no longer wishes to pay for the medical care of an elderly patient. However, assessing the value of life at its completion is different than the same assessment at its beginning. Valuing life for life's sake makes sense when that unborn life is only potential. Destroying life at its beginning rejects God's sovereign arrangement in creating it, abandons hope in God's sufficient grace and does not trust in God's ability to care for what he creates.

Life's sanctity, however, does not require its preservation at all costs when a lifetime is fulfilled. Those Christians who say the sanctity of life requires us to use any medical means to stay alive contribute to our inability to routinely teach and practice dying well. God is glorified when people die having lived a full life, accepting God's plan, hoping for continued life in Christ and trusting God to care for them in the journey from this life to the next. Many Christians who rightly reject euthanasia and physician-assisted suicide have promoted what one bioethicist calls "naive vitalism"—life at any cost.

A funeral director in Wheaton, Illinois, told me that the most common Bible verse families print on funeral bulletins or have read during services is 2 Timothy 4:7. They quote Paul saying, "I have fought the good fight." "Except," the director says, "they're not talking about spiritual things. They mean this person tried every medical option they could to stay alive."

Aggressive End-of-Life Care

While gradual dying gives us the advantage of advanced warning about the death, it is easy to squander the potential for end-of-life preparation. Aggressive medical care may always be our first option, but by pursuing powerful medicine until there is "nothing left to do" we likely forgo time with loved ones, final pursuits or perhaps a spiritual deepening in anticipation of life with God. There is a trade-off when choosing aggressive care, and we must learn to balance the proper desire for healing with the eventual need to die.

In response to end-of-life dramas like the 2005 case of Terri Schiavo and the acceptance among some doctors of physician-assisted suicide, the National Right to Life Committee offers a living will for anyone to use. The "Will to Live" is a legal document, like other living wills, that outlines what kind of medical treatment to use should the patient be unable to speak for him- or herself. The Will to Live asks doctors to do anything and everything to keep a patient alive. "Today, many doctors accept a 'quality of life' ethic," NRLC says in its explanation for why a Will to Live is necessary. "If they believe someone will have disabilities that make that person's life have too poor a quality, they will do everything they can to deny life-saving treatment and even food and water so the person will die."[11]

At best, this statement is inaccurate. Far from doctors denying life-saving treatment, as the NRLC claims, studies show that doctors and hospital staff regularly give patients more medical care than they want, treatment beyond their wishes. It would appear that patients and their physicians have difficulty acknowledging the inevitable. If only for liability reasons, doctors err on the side of overtreatment. One study that sought to reduce conflict between families and doctors found that the most common source of disagreement between doctors and patients was over the withdrawal of life support. A Duke University study of patients in the intensive care unit found that "three-quarters of those cases involved medical staff who wanted to continue treatment aggressively when the family did not."[12]

In one study, half of the patients who asked not to be resusci-

tated did not have Do Not Resuscitate (DNR) orders should their
hearts stop or they stop breathing. Unless patients have a Do Not
Resuscitate order in their charts, hospitals will always do everything they can to revive a deceased patient. The study found that
"only 47 percent of physicians knew when their patients preferred to avoid cardiopulmonary resuscitation." So, rather than
denying treatment to people who want it, doctors tend to assume patients desire all possible efforts to keep them alive.[13]

Another study found that patients, far from being denied care,
received more care than they wanted. "The final hospitalization
for half of patients included more than eight days in generally
undesirable states: in an ICU, on a ventilator, or in coma."[14] Patients and their families said they would have rather gone home
to die and forgone the medical care. Though less medical intervention means people may die sooner (though that is often not
the case), most people state in surveys that they would rather die
sooner at home than in a hospital bed, kept alive artificially—as
the Will to Live requires.

Despite NRLC's claims, it is doctors' tendency to overtreat
that leads people—fearing being mechanically kept alive—to
advocate for physician-assisted suicide. The horror of dying
hooked to machines is too often, though with good reason, our
image of death. The typical death in the hospital often comes
after invasive attempts to save the patient's life. Unfortunately,
in the ICU, that is how nearly half (45 percent) of deaths occur.[15]
One gerontologist told me that death today comes only after a
decision in its favor, because "there is always more we can do."
For those patients who cannot be kept alive by machines and
who do not have Do Not Resuscitate orders, their deaths will
typically follow one half hour of CPR. Such efforts might keep
someone alive, but the chances are slim and the costs are high.

The thirty-five thousand people currently in persistent vegetative states, says Stephen Kiernan, are there because life-saving efforts were able to revive a body, but not the person.[16] For most of these patients, death will come only after the removal of life support. The insistence on extensive medical care at the end of life often leads toward ethically dubious outcomes.

The medical community largely recognizes that attempts to legalize physician-assisted suicide are a condemnation of the way it handles dying. "Why would 750 people every year [in Oregon] decide that death for their loved ones was a merciful escape from the foreseeable medical options?" asks Kiernan. "They act on a violent combination of compassion and despair."[17] Unfortunately, many Christians insist—as a matter of faith and in order to be consistently pro-life—that all deaths should come only after deploying an arsenal of medical treatment. To many believers it seems paradoxical that one could at once be pro-life and embrace death as it approaches.

Gerontologist John Dunlop told me of an elderly patient dying of heart disease. Under the most optimistic scenario and best medical care, he said, she was weeks from death. The patient and her husband were Christians. Dunlop advised her to go home, say goodbye to her family, spend time with her loved ones and prepare herself spiritually. Instead, she requested to be transferred to a hospital in a nearby city, begging for a heart transplant.

"This dear lady," the doctor asks, "wants to live this way longer?" More important, her decision to pursue additional medical care made it impossible for her to prepare herself for the inevitable.

Dunlop, who practices geriatrics in Zion, Illinois, and teaches end-of-life ethics at Trinity Evangelical Divinity School, is critical of the way many Christians use medicine. "I view the practice of medicine as part of our taking dominion over the earth. It is part of God's way to reverse the curse," he says. "It's good. But not when we're shaking our fists in God's face and saying, 'No, I'm not going to die yet. I'm trusting technology to pull me through.'" Unfortunately, Dunlop says, among some Christians there is an expectation to act just that way.

A death that comes after heroic medical efforts does not allow for those things that Christians have traditionally sought in their own deaths and those of their loved ones. Throughout Christian history, Christians have sought to die well. A death that doesn't afford the opportunity for last words, for reconciliation, for repentance and for spiritual preparation for the next world is not a good death, according to traditional Christian teaching.

3

LOSING THE
CHRISTIAN DEATH

Instead of fighting death until the end, church history teaches us about the good death—one in which a believer seeks to faithfully express her hope in eternal life. It is a tragedy that the church has lost this vision of the good death. We are sending fellow believers into eternity unprepared for their journey. They may be sure of their destination but unsure how to get there. For Christians in previous centuries, death was a sacred moment long prepared for. It was considered one of the most important events in life, an event on which hung all of eternity. Christians took care to perform their dying faithfully. On their deathbeds they received family and friends who sat watch with the dying person, seeking evidence of their entrance to heaven.

Christians sought to learn from the dying because of their increased spirituality as they neared eternity. "Christians living in early modern England and America," writes pastor John Fanestil, "believed that the closer a person drew to the edge of death, the closer that person's soul was to God."[1] Deaths were recorded by family and friends and retold to those in the community who could not be present. The community drew comfort and encouragement from reports of those who crossed over in peace and hope. Preachers took the opportunity of a death to remind congregants of the source of death—sin—and its remedy through eternal life in Jesus Christ. In all these ways, people learned how to die well, so that when the time came, they were prepared.

Another feature of this tradition taught that the dead were a permanent part of church life. Centuries ago (and in some traditions that celebrate All Saints Day still today) the church saw itself made not only of the members who sat in the pews each sabbath but also those entombed believers awaiting the resurrection. The bodies of those Christians were often buried in the cemetery next to the church building, under its floor and inside its walls. The "communion of the saints" meant far more than pot luck dinners and small group fellowship.

For nineteen centuries Christians in different forms and different cultures understood that their attitude toward death should be infused with hope, for they worshiped a Lord who had defeated death. They died and cared for the dying differently than others in pre-Christian societies. Believers created the first hospitals and ended flippant attitudes toward the deaths of the unborn, newborn and elderly. They created organizations dedicated to caring for the dying poor and widows. The first Christians distinguished themselves in Roman society by remaining in the cities when epidemics struck, caring for the ill and burying the dead when the rest of society refused to touch anyone who was ill.[2] Though we modern Christians have undone their work, our early brothers and sisters in Christ brought cemeteries from outside of towns and cities into their center, integrating the community of the dead with that of the living.

But by the end of the nineteenth century the ground had been prepared for a radically new approach to death. According to historian Gary Laderman, during the nineteenth century "new ideas about science, medicine, and the life of the spirit contributed to a breakdown of religiously authoritative positions." Christian interpretations of death, he says, "were challenged, downplayed, or modified."[3]

Ideas about the judgment of God were difficult to sustain as scientists uncovered the causes of diseases that periodically rampaged through American communities. It was natural that superstitions about disease give way to scientific explanation, but in the exchange Americans radically reinterpreted divine action in the deaths of their loved ones. "By the twentieth century, to prepare [for death] was to vaccinate and filter water, not to ready one's soul for an unpredictable call," writes historian Robert Wells. "Once epidemics were understood to be secular problems and not God's judgment, it was possible to take action to remedy the worst conditions, but it was only another small step to make all deaths natural, devoid of spiritual significance."[4]

Unfortunately, not only were Christian interpretations of death marginalized by a country that had become more secular, but Christians themselves now looked differently on death. Letters from the first half of the twentieth century show a marked change in how Christians talked about death. They began to use strictly material terms. Christians used their faith not to understand death's meaning and purpose and prepare themselves for life eternal, but to provide comfort in grief. "She's gone to a better place," we now say. Death became not the inevitable result of sin but the natural process of journeying to heaven. "Much less commonly than at any other time in this millennium," says Sherwin Nuland, "do the dying nowadays turn to God and the promise of an afterlife when the present life is fading."[5]

Funeral sermons formerly coupled remembrance and grief over the death of a loved one with invitations to repent and share in the hope of resurrection and eternal life. This balance between the pain of death in this life and the joy of the divine resurrection life was ever present until it began to give way in the twentieth century. Donald Heinz, professor of religious studies at California State University, Chico, writes that during the twentieth century Christian denominations gave up long-held beliefs about death.

> Between 1836 and 1916 the Methodist funeral order, for example, maintained a delicate balance between fear and hope. After 1916, hope triumphed. The mercy of God and the assurance of everlasting life replaced God's power and wrath. Judgment, fear, and pain of death were eliminated.[6]

At least in the order of service.

Even the concept of heaven changed. It ceased to be the holding place of souls awaiting their bodily resurrection. Instead, writes historian Phillipe Aries, Christians created "a new paradise . . . which is not so much the heavenly home as the earthly home saved from the menace of time, a home in which the expectations of [heaven] are mingled with the realities of memory."[7] Rather than a place that could be spoken of only in metaphor, heaven became earth with intensified pleasure unmarred by any discomfort.

LACKING SPIRITUAL COMFORTS

Christians once saw a window to the next world as a fellow believer entered eternity. Visions of heaven, Jesus and family were once common on the deathbed. This provided faith-sustaining, hope-inducing and grief-allaying comfort to those who survived the death of a loved one.

Wells quotes a newspaper account of the 1817 death of Anna Vedder in Schenectady, New York.

> The newspaper remarked that the manner of her death was "not only calculated to sooth the grief of those by whom she was held dear in this life, but also to inculcate most strongly, upon the minds of all, the blessedness of those that die in the Lord." The paper assumed that "it cannot be uninteresting to hear that she died in the full assurance of faith. The candle of the Lord shone upon her head. Death had lost its sting. She walked over the waters of Jordan . . . shouting the praises of redeeming love. She declared, moreover, that she beheld a place, more splendidly decorated than the tongue of mortal could describe, wherein was a seat prepared for her."[8]

Such an expression that heaven was in view was once common and expected among Christians. Dallas Willard writes in *The Divine Conspiracy*,

> Before the widespread use of heavy sedation, it was quite common for those keeping watch to observe something like this. The one making the transition [dying] often begins to speak to those who have gone before. They come to meet us while we are still in touch with those left behind. The curtains part for us briefly before we go through.

After asking Willard about this passage, he told me of his own experience. "My brother, who died of Parkinson's, had been in a state of noncommunication for a long time. Just before he died,

he turned and said to his wife, 'Now, dear, you must let me go.'
And he went."

Those who work with the dying consistently report similar
stories. These range from accounts of angels and lights to sublime spiritual sensations. How would our faith be strengthened,
how would our grieving be eased if only we knew to look for
these things, and if we made medical decisions that would make
them possible? If Christians object to stories of angels or the miraculous attending someone's death, perhaps it is because they
have ceded that ground to spiritualists and New Age seekers,
who have then populated the territory with their own ideas.
Surely God is quite active at the deaths of his beloved, for precious in his sight are the deaths of his saints.

This is just one of many aspects of Christian dying I neglected
in my visits to my Aunt Eileen, but it is something I did discover
in my work as a hospice volunteer. With a renewed vision of the
Christian death, God might surprise us and comfort us with
what we discover in the experience of caring for the dying. These
kinds of experiences confirm Jesus' promise in John 14 to take
us to himself. And while I can't personally attest to supernatural
experiences at the deathbed, being among those near their deaths
has been a deeply spiritual experience.

Unfortunately, such stories never make it into our obituaries,
even in Christian publications. (I know; I've written several.)
We hide the deceased's final months and years. We list accom-
plishments, books written or organizations led. We measure the
subject's significance, and we quote the fond remembrances of
friends and loved ones. But we never mention how the subject
died, how he faced his end or how she prepared for the life to
come. Walter Wangerin Jr., a Lutheran pastor and author who
upon suffering from terminal cancer and facing his own death

complained about newspaper obituaries that describe battles with diseases, as if anyone ever wins. "Why not use the imagery that acknowledges how one experiences dying?—how one behaves in the face of death?—what one has to offer those who stand by in love and relationship?" Wangerin says.[9]

As the previous newspaper account illustrates, it used to be done. Anna Vedder was no one special, yet she was worth writing about not because of how she lived but how she died. Vedder seems to have orchestrated her death, "calculating" it to soothe the grief of her family and loved ones. Surely, this was a remarkable feat in an age when the dying felt the full, painful blow of an illness. Yet Mrs. Vedder took care to ease her loved ones' grief and to make sure they held on to the belief of "the blessedness of those that die in the Lord."

Mrs. Vedder gave that assurance by reporting what she witnessed as she "walked over the waters of Jordan." She might not have been able to shout praises, but she likely did offer praise as she looked upon a place "more splendidly decorated than the tongue of mortal could describe."

Even with today's heavy sedation, some people do witness their loved ones talking to people and seeing things that are not apparent. I have witnessed this myself when a hospice patient told me he'd had a strange visitor come to take him on a trip. It is scientifically accepted that the dying are sometimes able to know what reasonably they should not. For example, studies show that the dying are sometimes aware that a relative recently died, even when no one else in the family was aware of the death. "These mysteries imply that the boundary between life and death is not sharp for people dying gradually," writes Kiernan. "It is a blurry line, a transition zone. . . . People near the end appear to go back and forth, showing not anxiety but ease, a welcoming of what is to come."[10]

While we know little about what is actually happening, for Christians, it can be a faith-affirming comfort to witness a loved one glimpse what is beyond, to know they are headed into the company of saints and to know they embrace it. Stories of the dying and even of those with near-death experiences, such as the one told in *90 Minutes in Heaven,* can confirm the hope given to us in Scripture.

Of course, we cannot expect miraculous signs to attend every death. They are not promised us. John Wesley, who always asked his followers who were near death if they saw Jesus, never mentioned seeing Jesus at his own death. But Jesus did promise his followers this: "If I go and prepare a place for you, I will come back and take you to be with me" (John 14:3).

We Have No Christian Dying

There is an untapped reservoir of Christian belief about dying. Christians are people who claim to worship and have the life of the risen Son of God. A renewed practice of Christian dying should affect not just the dying and those caring for them, but will fundamentally affect church life and individual spiritual lives from beginning to end.

For example, I have prayed in church and in prayer groups for the sick and the terminally ill. I've always felt obliged to pray for a miracle, that God would use the opportunity of a person's severe illness to disrupt the apparent laws of nature and display his power. But, eventually, praying this way became discouraging because those miracles never came. Slowly, I began—I thought—to pray more realistically. Instead of asking for a miracle, I prayed simply for grace and comfort from the Holy Spirit for the patient and his or her family. I prayed for wisdom when deciding among treatment options, and I prayed for those treatments to be effective. When they were not, I fell silent.

Yet my so-called realistic prayers were not really better prayers. I never prayed that someone would die well, as a faithful Christian. I never prayed that a death would bring about an opportunity for reconciliation and completion in relationships, or for God to bring something good from this evil. I never asked God to smooth someone's entrance to eternity. I know better now. "The idea that deaths can be inspirational—even redemptive—almost never enters modern conversations about death," writes John Fanestil, "yet this understanding lies at the core of the Christian gospel."[11]

"You have to work hard to avoid discussions of dying in the church," says C. Ben Mitchell, a former professor at Trinity Evangelical Divinity School and head of the Center for Bioethics and Human Dignity, and now teaching at Union University. "Yet that's exactly what we've done. We have avoided it with all of our might."

Ironically, Mitchell says, "Of all groups of people, Christians should be able to face dying well. After all, at the heart of our confession is a Redeemer who died."

If we thought about and practiced a ritual of Christian dying, what would it look like? What should a Christian caregiver do for a loved one nearing death? If we look at how medicine can help us achieve those goals, rather than assessing what treatments are right and wrong, we could take dying out of the culture wars and put it back into the category of normal spiritual disciplines alongside prayer and fasting. Christians could then provide examples to a culture desperately searching for a way to deal with death.

For the dying person spiritual issues are paramount. And the spiritual preparation necessary for a good, faithful death accumulates slowly over a lifetime. A good death does not occur in a vacuum. Also necessary are a supportive family and caring spiritual community alongside a medical community able to provide quality care consistent with the goals of a patient. Achieving this kind of community, of a similar mind, can happen as a church and family rallies to the side of an ill member—when everything goes well. Often it does not. Developing a community united about the values we should bring to the deathbed rarely happens in the midst of a medical crisis. It grows slowly as we hear sermons and share stories, as we care for one another and think alone of the fact that one day we too will die.

When we do that, we will have truly set our minds on heaven. The church, more than anything else, is a community that believes in the resurrection of the dead—first that of our Lord Jesus Christ, to be followed by the resurrection of those who believe in him and the re-creation of the world. Our faith has this-world consequences in how we treat our neighbors, how we behave at work, how we relate to our families, how we care for loved ones nearing death. If our faith has any earthly consequence, then certainly it should affect how we practice our deaths.

We have a tremendous opportunity thanks to medical advances that brought about the gradual death, and we have a frightful task. Our church friends, our loved ones and we ourselves are unlikely to be taken by surprise by a sudden death. We have the time to decide how we will face it. We have the chance to help others pass from death, as it slowly advances, into new life. It takes bravery and some fortitude to tell someone you love, "When I die, this is what I want."

I found that it wasn't easy to tell my wife that while I hope to live to an old age, whatever point in life that I am struck by an accident or illness likely to end it, I want to be in hospice for at least a few months before I die. I want my heath care decisions to be guided by my desire to spend a good deal of time in comfort and peace so that I'm able to give my thoughts to God, my family and loved ones. As difficult as the conversation was, I found it helpful to start. I know it's one we'll have many times over our lifetime together as we age and our lives and health change.

On the other hand, I've so far failed to have the same conversation in significant depth with my parents. It takes a strong willingness to bring up such an uncomfortable topic. It pains me to think of my wife or my parents suffering in a hospital bed. I don't want to ask them: How do you want to die? Would you ever want me to remove life support? What do you want to accomplish before you do? What spiritual resources will you need?

Yet, if we don't ask these questions, either our doctors, our insurers or hospital staff will make these decisions for those we love. If our churches don't teach what Christian dying should be, if our pastors are afraid to come to our bedsides, if our loudest voices care about passing laws, then we forfeit the opportunity to practice the spiritual discipline of dying well. Our deaths will then be guided by the prevailing winds of our health care system.

We surely will die—most likely in old age but by no means necessarily so. It is good to think about that throughout our lives, the Bible says. We are wise to learn to number our days. We can be thankful that medicine has given us the expectation—though no guarantee—of long lives to prepare ourselves. We, in turn, can look at the cross and the empty tomb in hope and trust in our God who "raised Christ Jesus from the dead." And we hope and believe that in the last day, we too will be bodily resurrected. As the Bible promises: "he will give life to your mortal bodies" (Romans 8:11 NLT).

4

THE INDIVIDUAL, THE CHURCH
AND *ARS MORIENDI*

In late winter during the fifty-ninth year of his life,
John Donne braved the weather and rough roads of the English
countryside to keep his final preaching engagement before the
king in London. He had spent most of that winter, what would
be his last, battling "consumption," and on several occasions he
nearly died. But he was eager to simply preach again. Donne had
grown to love his midlife calling as a preacher. Better known
today and early in his own life as a poet of love, Donne was also
an exquisite expositor.

Throughout his life, Donne was a very public figure in London. His poetry circulated widely, passed and copied from hand
to hand. As a young man, his earliest verses spoke of a wild dec-
adence—trysts with women and overseas adventures. But public
scorn of his elopement followed by years without steady work
sobered his spirit. Years later, when the king offered him a position as a priest in the Church of England, Donne accepted. He
was wildly successful in his new career and became even more

prominent in London society. So, when Donne performed his death, he performed it as he had lived—as though on a stage or written into a poem.

An often sickly man, it is no surprise that much of Donne's writing dealt with death. Meditating on death was nothing new to Donne. His famous Elegies poetically address death and dying. And his popular *Devotions Upon Emergent Occasions* are his reflections after nearly dying from plague as it raged through London. Yet Donne never wanted to publish his poetry, for which he is better known. During his final illness, Donne compiled and edited his sermons for publication. As if he were arranging them for posterity to be sure the world knew how he valued his preaching, Donne devoted his healthy hours to this final task.

As he lay ill, preparing his sermons (some of which would have lasted four hours if delivered aloud), Donne also made out his will.[1] Before divvying up his possessions, Donne began his will with a statement of his faith, saying that he remained assured through the Holy Spirit "of the Salvation of [his soul], and the Resurrection of [his body]."[2] Finally, having tied up his earthly affairs and prepared what he hoped would be his legacy, his sermons, Donne was ready to travel to preach to England's elite.

After months of illness and more than half a year spent away from London, Donne's friends were shocked by his appearance upon his return. They were astonished, as his biographer described, that Donne's illness left him just "so much flesh as did only cover his bones." They doubted whether he would be able to perform the upcoming service and did their best to persuade him not to attempt it as it was likely to quicken his death.[3] They proved correct, but Donne would not listen.

Donne rose before his audience at the king's court, believing that God, having kept him alive so long, would not yet withdraw his strength. The crowd, amazed simply at his presence, according to his biographer, thought Donne had traveled to London not to "preach mortification by a living voice, but mortality by a decayed body, and a dying face."

Though Donne paused on occasion, weak from his effort, he determined to deliver the sermon he had worked so hard—in mind and body—to prepare. To many in the congregation, it seemed Donne was preaching for his own benefit as much as theirs.

The sermon was a sensation. It was quickly printed under the title "Death's Duel." In it, Donne seems to be readying himself for his imminent departure from this life, and he instructs his listeners to do the same.

"Our birth dies in infancy, and our infancy dies in youth, and youth and the rest die in age," Donne told the court. Physical death, he argues, may even be welcomed, for it is easier than life. "So many deadly calamities accompany every condition and every period of this life, as that death itself would be an ease to them that suffer them."

We need not worry too much about the painful affects of disease that dying unleashes. After all, God himself is in control of our leaving this world, Donne said, and it is his concern how we leave. So we may trust in him. "Though . . . we pass from death to death, yet, as Daniel speaks, the Lord our God is able to deliver us, and he will deliver us."

Facing death with assurance and hope however is no easy task. And if we fail, we need not worry, because it is not death, Donne says, that makes the Christian. "It is not the last stroke that fells the tree, nor the last word nor gasp that qualifies the soul." Our Lord will still care for us and accept us even if our courage fails.

So we pray "for [a] time of repentance against sudden death, and
for sober and modest assurance against" pain and difficulty in
dying.

It is not the process of our exit that leads to eternity with
God, Donne says, but our whole Christian life. "God doth not
say, Live well, and thou shalt die well, that is an easy, a quiet
death; but Live well here, and thou shalt live well for ever." So
our efforts are to be spent in Christian living. "Our critical day
is not the very day of our death, but the whole course of our
life."

The extraordinary death of Christ, Donne says, is our example in dying. "That God, this Lord, the Lord of life, could die, is
a strange contemplation." And yet, "He would not spare, nay, he
could not spare himself," and if it is fitting for God himself to die
as a man, it is proper for us his creatures to die as well. And
therefore, "To us that speak daily of the death of Christ . . . can
the memory or the mention of our own death be irksome or
bitter?"

Finally, Donne says, as Jesus Christ gave up his spirit, we must
also be ready to die. "There we leave you in that blessed depen-
dency, to hang upon him that hangs upon the cross . . . till he
[grant] you a resurrection, and an ascension into that kingdom
which He hath prepared for you with the inestimable price of his
incorruptible blood. Amen."

THE CHRISTIAN ART OF DYING

Since the beginning of the church Christians have cared for the
dying and sought to practice their deaths in ways that express belief in Christ's death and his resurrection. These practices sought
to honor the body as the image of God. If God became a human,
and even he had to die, Christians recognized that to die is not

something to fight against, though it was not a part of God's original design. And if Christ was raised from death, Christians believe that death does not hold any power over the faithful.

Donne was immersed in a culture that prepared even its children to die well, expressing these Christian values and beliefs. Medieval Christians contemplated their own deaths early and often. Disease struck the young and old without warning. "Life, men thought then, was a preparation for death, and it behooved each one to be ready to meet it," writes one of Donne's biographers. "The surest way to meet such a moment was to have been through it often in the mind, to have endured it all in anticipation, and so to be able to meet it with the confidence becoming a Christian who trusted in the saving grace of Christ's sacrifice."[4]

This mental preparation resulted in the *ars moriendi,* the art of dying. Christians in the second half of the fifteenth century endured their deaths in anticipation of the resurrection with the help of illustrated woodcuts. At that time the plague raged through Europe, and Christians could no longer count on the support of others at the end of their lives. Priests typically cared for the dying, administering the last rites, but during the plague, writes historian Arthur Imhof, "many people died at the same time, and there were not enough priests to assist everyone." These widely circulated woodcuts provided a way to minister to people who were alone.[5]

Knowing they were likely to die alone, individuals were compelled by the church to learn to die. Woodcut pictures depicted the deathbed scene, with the dying man surrounded by either devils or angels, or both, vying for the soul. Like stained-glass images in church, the woodcuts told a story. They illustrated both the temptations one would meet in the face of death (impatience, fear, etc.) and the means to overcome them. The wood-cuts were followed by explanations on the art of dying, to be used by priests or anyone else who could read. For those who couldn't, the pictures were instruction enough. The *ars moriendi* booklets were extremely popular, and more than three hundred Latin and vernacular editions were eventually printed.[6] Beginning with this single book of pictures, the larger tradition of *ars moriendi* developed—a Christian practice as well as a literary tradition instructing the faithful on how to die.

While this small picture book provides an example of how Christians sought to learn and practice good deaths, it was just the first of many manuals Christians used to practice and prepare for their deaths. As the tradition developed, a number of common themes emerged, tying different rituals and practices together:

- Death requires preparation.
- The dying process is a deeply spiritual event.
- Death is to be actively undertaken.
- Death is a public and instructive event.
- Death injures the community.

The *ars moriendi* tradition blossomed not only because of the emergence of the plague but also because Christian tradition asserted that the death of a follower of Christ was to be different from those who die without faith. This life is only the prelude to an eternal life with Christ. We, like Jesus, will be reunited with our glorified bodies. We will worship God corporately for eternity. So we have reason to hope and to be in peace as our life on earth comes to its end.

And we also have an example in Christ's death, which we can

follow. God in the flesh died—strange indeed, as Donne wrote. Yet Jesus showed us how to die. He was tormented, as any human would be, by the prospect of his death, yet he went willingly. He took care of his family and their earthly concerns, even as he died, by asking his follower to look after his mother. He gave up his spirit, and so willingly and actively participated in his dying. "From the very outset," wrote the Catholic theologian Jean-Charles Didier,

> Christians were aware . . . how much death changed its aspect when seen through Christ, who had himself conquered death and saved the world by his own dying. The death of Christ appeared in very truth to his followers as the greatest act of love, the ideal passage from the world to God, the perfect sacrifice on behalf of all mankind, and his glorious resurrection projected its light through the gate he had opened.[7]

Throughout Christian history, Christians intentionally practiced their own deaths, cared for the dying and prepared for their passing in ways that reflected their beliefs about the life and death of Jesus Christ.

It is clear from Christian history that dying well requires preparation. Jesus not only prepared himself, most intensively in the garden on the night before he died, but he also tried to prepare his followers. In previous centuries, children—who were often as likely to die as their elders—learned nursery rhymes that reminded them of the transitory nature of their life on earth. English children sang alphabet rhymes like "X: Xerxes the great did die / And so must you and I," and "Y: Youth forward slips / Death soonest nips."[8] And they prayed each night before laying down to slumber, which so closely resembles death: "Now I lay me down to sleep. I pray the Lord my soul to keep. And if I die before I wake, I pray the Lord my soul to take."

This emphasis on preparing to die encouraged Christians to live throughout life with eternity in mind. The prospect of death focuses the mind on our priorities. So good deaths naturally followed good lives. Dying was too terrible an event to face unprepared, but a lifetime of Christian living helped to get one ready. When death did come, either suddenly or by a preparing sickness, the Christian could accept it in peace and hope. "All that a sick and dying man can do, is but to exercise those virtues which he before acquired," wrote Jeremy Taylor in his *Holy Dying*,[9] a classic text in the *ars moriendi* tradition.

Preparation for death did not diminish its agonies, but Christians knew that death's "pain and suffering would be accompanied in equal measure by happiness and blessing" for both the dying and survivors alike, writes John Fanestil, a pastor whose ministry has been shaped by the deaths of his parishioners. "The deathbed," writes Fanestil of the early Methodist tradition of the happy death, "was the last, and most important, venue for practicing the way of the cross."[10]

REFORMING THE ART OF DYING

In centuries gone by, Christians acknowledged that the dying process is a deeply spiritual event. Today, those who have been able to be present at the death of a loved one often agree, describing it as a spiritual experience. Yet Scripture tells us very little about the life to come or what precisely Jesus meant when he promised to come to take us to himself.

As a result, anxiety is natural and common among Christians. Even though the Bible assures us of our destiny, getting there can be frightening. A hospice patient once told me about his ailments:

a bad heart and colon cancer. "And now they've got me in hospice," he said with obvious concern. "So I don't know what's next." He looked at me plaintively, but it was clear we both knew what was next. The thought of his death was visibly worrisome to him. He then asked me to pray for him. "That's the best thing, you know!" he said. A lifelong, active Christian who said he looked forward to being in heaven, this patient was still concerned about the process of dying.

The same was true even for those medieval Christians who learned the *ars moriendi*. Though the deathbed scene, when peaceful, comforted onlookers, it was not always serene. In fact, "horror and fear are the emotions most commonly associated with late medieval perceptions of death and the life everlasting," writes Eamon Duffy in *The Stripping of the Altars,* "and preachers, dramatists, and moralists did not hesitate to employ terror . . . to stir their audiences to penitence and good works."[11]

But their exhortations may have been overused. The first Reformers, says Austra Reinis, in her study of German Reformation *ars moriendi,* sought to assure their followers of the certainty of their salvation rather than use the fear of death to encourage good works. It was only natural, the Reformers said, for Christians to be fearful of death. Yet they did not need to gird themselves for spiritual warfare. The spiritual process of dying simply involved resting in the faith of Christ's victory on the cross.[12] Having experienced the joy of salvation during their life, Christians could rest in Christ's work—confident of entrance to heaven and joyful, no matter the final terrors.

Martin Luther's "Sermon on Preparing to Die" best reflects this return to the practice of being joyful in Christ during the spiritual process of dying. Luther wrote the sermon at the request of a friend who was worried about his death, and Luther shaped the sermon in a way that would calm the fears of his friends and followers as they looked into the eyes of death. Rather than encourage his readers to immediately repent and ask for God's forgiveness, Luther begins his sermon by acknowledging "the fear that a dying person experiences." He encourages his readers "to joyfully and confidently embark on the path toward God."[13] "The emotional peace and calm that the Christian derives from contemplating the counter-image of the living Christ is in stark contrast to the emotional condition of the 'worried, weak and hopeless' Christian who at the point of death dwells on the evil image of death."[14]

In the first paragraphs of his sermon, Luther sets a distinct tone, distinguishing his "Sermon on Preparing to Die" from the prior *ars moriendi* literature. The deathbed is a place to rest in Christ, says Luther, not battle the forces of evil. This is a spiritual process, turning our attention from matters of this world to those of the next. The deathbed is the culmination of the Christian life, not its cataclysmic scene. Rather than cast the dying person in the decisive position of choosing between the five temptations or five virtues, Luther contrasted the "images" of death, sin and hell against life, grace and heaven. Luther encouraged his followers to take communion as a sign which would remind the dying person "that Christ's victory over the evil powers of death, sin and hell is also the Christian's victory."[15] For centuries the church had urged Christians to take communion at their death, sometimes even encouraging believers to receive the bread at the moment of expiration.[16] Luther continued the tradition, but he taught that the sacrament was only a visible reminder of the work of Christ, not a magical key to eternity. So, the dying Christian need not worry if a priest was unavailable to serve communion—though he urged priests to stay with the dying even in the face of the plague. Whether or not a priest arrived, however, Christ's death was still valid and applicable by faith.

While the Reformers adapted the traditional *ars moriendi* to their theology, they still insisted on the importance of the spiritual process of dying. Christians were to be actively and spiritually involved as their souls separated from their bodies to join Jesus. Reformers encouraged the dying to thank God when they did not suffer a sudden death. A slow death allowed the Christian to take the sacraments, confess, pray and otherwise prepare themselves and their soul.[17]

A DYING FACE

The early *ars moriendi* taught that the spirit of the Christian was quite alive, wrestling with angels and demons, even as the body died. Therefore, death was to be actively undertaken. Though Christians changed in their beliefs about what happens at the moment of death, they never dismissed the idea that the spirit was still active.

Modern science teaches that in the process of dying, when death is not caused by trauma, a body actually shuts itself down. It does not simply stop working. Rather, organs prepare themselves to cease their function, like a factory closing shop by turning off the machines and sweeping before cutting the power. So our body, even while dying, is still working. In the same way, the spirit of the Christian is too.

For example, hospice workers often report seemingly strange events which, for them, are proof of purposeful living even in a dying person. Some wait hours or even days until they are alone before dying. Other times, those who are extremely ill may appear to doctors to be physically unable to live, without blood pressure or signs of breathing, yet they stay alive until certain

words are spoken or certain visitors arrive who perhaps offer
reconciliation or permission to die.

What nurses and doctors recognize today, Christians understood centuries ago. When medical techniques to prolong life
were not available, says pastor John Fanestil, people were not so
passive about their dying.

> Those who practiced the ritual of happy dying near the
> turn of the nineteenth century . . . did not approach it in a
> spirit of resignation or despair. To the contrary, because
> they believed God's hands were strong and trustworthy,
> [they] embraced death, or, better yet, they rose to greet it
> as if rushing into a loving embrace.[18]

No one assumed that the difficult physical work of dying would
leave a person spiritually unable to participate.[19]

This was true of Donne's death. After delivering "Death's
Duel," he returned to his apartment and ordered his affairs. He
invited his friends and said goodbye individually to each. And
finally, he prayed and looked to God for deliverance.

He found a unique means of focusing those prayers during his
final weeks. Though today we might find it morbid, Donne's last
days were widely admired during his lifetime, and they show the
great lengths to which people went in order to die well.

At the request of friends, Donne posed for an artist to draw
his portrait, which would then be used to make a statue of Donne
after his death. Donne was quite ill, and rather than trying to
look his best, he tied a burial shroud over his body and stood
upon an urn. Donne was telling everyone that he was prepared
and ready for eternity. The statue made still stands in St. Paul's
Cathedral. Donne took the drawing and set it by his bed. For
hours a day he used the picture to meditate upon his death and

pray to God until he no longer had strength and the God Donne so loved received him.

A PUBLIC EVENT

As bells tolled across England and Europe announcing another death from the plague, Christians were reminded at every moment that death was a public event and instructive to the church. While death was a spiritual event, according to Christian tradition, it was and is not a private affair simply between a Christian and God. Indeed, the loss of a single brother or sister in Christ wounded deeply the community of faith. "No man is an island," wrote Donne in his *Devotions,* "every man is a piece of the continent."

Two characteristics of death in the Middle Ages, says historian Phillipe Aries in his one-thousand-year history of Western attitudes of dying, lasted until the end of the nineteenth century: its familiar simplicity and public nature. "The dying person must be the center of a group of people," says Aries. As late as "the early nineteenth century, when the last sacrament was being taken to a sick man, anyone could come into the house and into the bedroom, even if he was a stranger to the family."[20]

The public dimension of death was so strongly held that Frederick Paxton in his history *Christianizing Death* writes of a group of priests in the early Middle Ages who pledged to ritually care for each other in sickness and death. "When one of the fraternity fell ill," Paxton writes, "the others were to congregate at his house, sing the seven penitential psalms along with a litany and prayers, and bless holy water." They would then go to the church and say mass for the sick member, returning again to share bread and water. If the sickness lasted a while, the fraternity would continue the ritual for twelve days; after which only one member would visit until death seemed immanent.[21] The moments before death were filled with caregivers and friends anointing the dying one, standing vigil, commending the spirit to God and preparing the body. Even after death, he would be remembered in masses and prayers, at first daily following burial, then monthly and annually.[22]

As anyone who has observed a good death can attest, it is in many ways a life-changing event for those watching. While tremendously sad and even horrible, a good death can also be beautiful and deeply moving. Such deaths were to be shared by members of the Christian community who were thereby encouraged in their faith. When death is public it is harder for the rest of us to become afraid of it. There is less mystery as we see how the physical body ceases to function. There is less fear as we see caregivers assist the dying in their last moments. There is more hope as we watch, even for a moment, the veil lifted and a dying person drawn into eternity. When we've seen a friend or loved one die, it's easier to learn to die. We can rehearse in our minds our own death, we learn what to do when others who we love face death, and we live better lives with eternity in mind.

In the days that preceded Mona's death, she was visited often in the rehab center by family members. Her children sat at her bedside and prayed with her. Death by Alzheimer's comes in increments, and Mona had been dying for more than five years now. On the day before she died, two of her daughters came to visit for what, they would learn, was their last time. They sang hymns and held her hands as she squirmed in her bed, pulling at her hospital nightgown. Her youngest daughter offered her a drink and, when the aide came with dinner, sat beside the bed and spoon-fed her mother.

"As I sat holding Mom's hand, I kept saying over and over, 'You're okay, Mom. It's okay, Mom,'" Michelle told me. Looking across the bed at her sister spoon-feeding the mother who had once spoon-fed them, Michelle began to cry. "I remembered all of the times she had cared for me. Now it was my turn to give that care in return. We did all the things for her that she had done for us all of her life. We fed her and comforted and reassured her with our words and touch.

"I had never been with a dying person before Mom got sick," Michelle said. "But when I think about it now, caring for Mom wasn't all that different from how I cared for my kids when they were babies—or how Mom cared for me when I was little. I hope I helped to make her last moments as love-filled as she made my first moments after I had entered the world."

A Beautiful Injury

As Donne's final weeks attest, he remained spiritually alive even as his body neared death. He eagerly awaited and looked for his entrance to life with God. He prayed, and having let go of things on earth, began to clutch those of heaven.

Yet, while Donne died well, those who loved him still mourned. Good deaths, even the best of them, are terrible because they separate—if only temporarily—people who have intertwined their lives. So, Christian history teaches us, the good death still injures the community. Death, even the good or happy death, is a painful event. It is evil and not a part of God's creation, though God can bring good from it. And those closest to the deceased, in particular, need their wounds healed.

Funerals and other Christian rituals following death are meant, in large part, to nurse those wounds and reunite a community that has fractured. Phillipe Aries describes the classic Western Christian behaviors when the member of a community died. It "solemnly altered space and time," he says. Shutters were

closed and other visible signals outside the house alerted neighbors to what was happening inside. Candles were lit, prayers
said, and clergy visited and performed their rites to bind the
wounds of the mourning. Neighbors and relatives visited, and
when death occurred tolling bells marked the significant loss of
a member of the community.

The body or coffin was displayed outside, or later just a notice
hung from the door of the house, and in came the neighborhood.
They brought food or simply their best wishes, and the bereaved
began their reintegration into the community without their
loved one. At a church service everyone gathered, remembered
the deceased and expressed their sympathy. They then processed
to the cemetery. This ritual pilgrimage gave those in sorrow the
means by which to enact their grief and articulate their inex-
pressible loss. There was safety and comfort in numbers; no one
was left to grieve alone.

A period of mourning would be filled with visits, Aries says:
"Visits of the family to the cemetery and visits of relatives and
friends to the family." Slowly, life regained its sense of normalcy.
"The social group had been stricken by death, and it had reacted
collectively, starting with the immediate family and extending
to a wider circle of relatives and acquaintances."[23] Such practices
were the normal and generally understood rituals that Christians performed for a thousand years throughout Western Christianity, Aries says. These rituals were done to mark death, instruct the living community on the Christian understanding of
death and offer the hope of bodily resurrection.

Today these rituals are often criticized on the grounds of being expensive or too much of a bother. We complain that funerals are unnecessary, that caskets and all the accouterments of
death are the cruel exploitation of the grieving. Many modern

mourners don't like the idea of funerals at all. They host parties in honor of a person who is simply unable to attend. One funeral director says the job should be more like that of an event planner.[24] This is what consumers want. A death is sometimes just another excuse to party, since that is what the deceased valued in life, and funerals are simply too sad.

Yet what we do after someone dies matters, and not only because the value we place on memorializing someone reflects our value of the person. Christian funerals, of course, may be joyous celebrations. But whether somber or celebratory, faithful believers must gather to remember and honor their deceased brothers and sisters. Through these rituals the injured community acknowledges its loss, instructs the living and begins the difficult process of rebuilding. A funeral begins the reintegration of a mourning believer into the community of Christians. It reinforces the belief that the deceased has gone to be with God, which is the same destiny for all Christians. And it offers hope that just as Christ rose from the grave, so will we rise again. A funeral service does all this in a way that worships God—whether by somber reflection or joyful, hand-clapping celebration—for his salvation and wisdom. In this way also the funeral instructs the community on the nature of death, an evil God has defeated and from which God can bring good.

THE CHRISTIAN ART OF DYING

Christians throughout history have attempted to practice their deaths in a way that reflects their faith. "The dying person in the Christian tradition is invited to immerse—as she or he did in baptism—a human story in a divine story, the Christian's dying in the paschal mystery of Christ's death and resurrection," says Donald Heinz.[25] The practice began with Christ's first followers, was emphasized by the martyrs, ritualized by the monastics and popularized by the *ars moriendi*. The tradition of the art of dying continued in various forms until the end of the nineteenth century. By that time a set of beliefs about the art of dying held true throughout Christianity.

The Christian art of dying is not a denial of the awfulness of death. In fact, Christians recognize, as Paul did, that death is the last enemy. The Christian tradition of *ars moriendi* recognized that horror and provided the tools that can help to guide believers through their last hours. The Christian death is an embodiment of a belief in a God who has defeated death and will give life to our own mortal bodies. As we care for the dying and make choices about our own last days, we stand positioned to regain a deeper understanding of this eternal triumph and the hope of Christ's resurrection.

5

THE SPIRITUALITY
OF DYING

Because of his Alzheimer's, my hospice patient, Edward, and I were never able to communicate well. I would get off the elevator in the convalescence center, look around the tables where the elderly and ill residents occupied themselves with simple games, slept or watched the activities outside. Each week for a year I scanned the tables and looked for Edward, leaned over in his wheelchair asleep.

I usually woke him up, knowing I was one of his only visitors and that he'd be glad to have someone to talk to. I'd ask Edward questions, and he would mumble answers. Sometimes he would talk very intelligibly, and I understood every word. But even then his mind was confused. I understood his words, but they made no sense. Even on good days I could never play much of a role in the conversation. I often simply nodded agreement with him and asked Edward to tell me more.

Though we could never carry on a meaningful conversation, I continued to visit, and over the course of a few months I thought Edward began to appreciate my presence. There was never anything particularly special about our relationship, but he would smile as I arrived and tell me it was good to see me and to have a good day when I left. I discovered that Edward enjoyed it when I simply blathered on about anything and everything that came to mind. Doing this is no skill of mine, but it didn't seem to matter to Edward. I would talk about my kids or upcoming travel plans. I'd talk about work, about the weather, about Chicago's sports teams.

On one occasion I was talking about a recent vacation, and I decided to ask Edward if he'd gone on any trips, though I knew he never left the convalescence center. It didn't matter; I figured that he might tell me about some vacation he'd taken with his family years before.

Edward said he did, indeed, expect a visitor. "A guy's coming to get me."

"Really," I said, glad he was talking. "Who is he?"

"I don't know. We just met a little while ago."

Edward had been sleeping when I arrived, as he often did, so I wondered who he could have just met. "Is he still here?" I asked looking around the room.

We were sitting in the room in which Edward spent most of his days. He raised his bony finger and pointed a couple tables away from where we sat. "He's over there." There were plenty of people in the room with us. The folks at the convalescent center had just finished lunch, and some people were sleeping in wheelchairs and others were just staring out the window.

But nobody was sitting in the direction Edward pointed.

"What's his name?" I asked.

Edward looked up at me with a big smile. "His name is Passover." They were the clearest words he had ever spoken to me.

"When is he coming to get you?"

Edward paused. "I hope never," he said, then smiled again.

Edward seemed comfortable with this man's presence, and though Edward's reaction suggested he wasn't yet ready to go on a journey with the stranger, Edward was comfortable with the idea of leaving with him.

A friend who works in the intensive care unit of a Chicago hospital told me she has seen many similar scenes—inexplicable and mysterious occurrences happen as people die. Others have described feeling a spiritual presence at someone's death, as if the person who died were still there. Still others tell of loved ones talking to already-deceased family members as they neared death, as if dead loved ones had come to assist in the journey home.

There is nothing in the Bible to explain precisely who or what Edward was pointing to, assuming he wasn't simply deluded. Perhaps it was an angel or Jesus come to help Edward on his trip to heaven, or a vision. Such an explanation would be consistent with Christian teaching. But while the Bible does not tell us precisely what happens at death—leaving us with latitude to make our own interpretations—the important fact is that spiritually a dying person is very much alive. Edward, despite his mind having been ravaged by Alzheimer's, knew that he wasn't yet ready to go on one last journey with Passover.

The spiritual dimension of a person who outwardly is wasting away is still quite active, alert and aware of its spiritual environment. We often think of spiritual growth at the end of life involving a new self-awareness—a new understanding of the spiritual life or a reinvigorated devotional life. But our spiritual life is more than psychological personal growth. Even Alzheimer's can't touch the life of the spirit. When a dying person gives physical evidence that his or her spirit is entering a new life, it can be spiritually encouraging to onlookers and emotionally comforting to those who will grieve the loss of the person. And as we support the dying spiritually, we help them to die well.

THE VETERAN

Paul, a World War II veteran, was dying of complications from diabetes. A father of four girls and one boy, he lived with his family in Wisconsin. After the war, he worked to raise his large Catholic family. However, those memories of the war remained an important part of his life and eventually his death.

Becky, one of Paul's daughters, said that even in his old age he remained close to his army buddies. "He had several guys from his hometown that were all in the service with him. They all made it through, and they remained friends throughout their lives." Dinners together with their families, as the friends aged, turned into breakfasts of donuts and coffee. Growing up, Becky would listen to her father's stories and the faith he had in God, who Paul believed provided very real protection from harm during the war. Though he dodged bullets in Europe, diabetes slowly caught up with him. He entered a local hospice program, but stayed alive much longer than expected. "He just hung on," Becky says.

And just when it seemed that Paul's life would soon end, the family's hospice nurse had to leave. For her own reasons she was taking another job. It devastated Becky and her family. "She worked for a long time with him," Becky said. "Dad was at least a couple months in hospice, and they got to know the nurse. They really grew to love her. She was a source of strength for the family at that time."

The nurse was leaving despite the fact that Paul had only days of life left. Hospice staff told Becky's mother to call her children and let them know their father would soon die. "My mom was really upset about the nurse leaving, and my dad too," Becky says.

Paul had told the family he wanted to die at home, and they made sure he could. After hospice suggested Paul would probably soon die, Becky's family came home, and they had nearly all arrived on the day of the new hospice nurse's first shift. The family was in the living room where Paul's bed was. "The new hospice person comes to the door," Becky says, "and he walked in and introduced himself to all of us. He walked over to my father, and he said, 'Paul, I'm Jeff, and I was a soldier myself. I served in Vietnam, and I've come as one brother to another to carry you home.'"

Suddenly, the family's apprehensions about the new hospice nurse were gone. "That was all my dad needed to hear. It was like a connection right away."

The nurse then turned to the family and asked if they were Christians. Becky's family all said they were believers. "Paul is on a journey," he told them, "and his journey's nearly ending. He's on his way home."

Becky says, "We almost thought God sent an angel to actually carry him and be with him. He was wonderful." As Paul grew closer to death, Becky's sense of divine intervention would only increase.

Typically very private about their faith, the family prayed together and read Scripture that night. As they read, Becky's sister, the only family member who hadn't arrived yet, flew in from her home in Norway.

It was early February, just two weeks from her parents' anniversary on Valentine's Day. Without her mother knowing, Becky and her siblings helped her dad sign a Valentine's card. "He was so weak that we had to move his hand," Becky says, "and try and help him sign this card." Later, at her mother's request, Becky tried to test his blood sugar. Though she squeezed Paul's finger, no blood came out. His feet had turned cold and dark. Becky knew that he would die soon, if not that night.

As the family got ready for bed, Becky said she thought someone should stay up with her father. Since she was wide awake, Becky offered to take the first shift along with her sister from Norway, who, jet-lagged, wasn't ready to sleep either.

As it got late, Becky noticed that her father, who just hours earlier had been too weak to sign a card for his wife, suddenly seemed alert and looking around the room. Becky's sister said he looked as though he were seeing someone, and the two sat quietly trying not to disturb their father.

Paul continued to look around the room, his eyes darting back and forth. Eventually, Becky's sister wanted to talk to her father and assure herself that he was ready for heaven. "I want to know that he believes in Jesus," she said. Paul responded to his daughter with both certainty and delight, "Oh, yes, I believe in Jesus." It was unusually convincing, Becky said, from someone who had been so private about his beliefs. After praying with him, the sisters sat back down to wait out the night.

Becky continued to watch her father, because he once again began looking all around the room. "It was odd for me to see what he was doing, looking around like he was seeing something. Even though he was very weak, all of a sudden I saw him reach up and yank the oxygen off his face."

Paul's breathing became very labored. Becky asked her father if he wanted her to put the oxygen back on. He told her no. "I knew that he knew right where he was going. He was ready. He was on his way. It was like he had one foot in eternity and one foot out."

Then, Paul's behavior changed again. "He began to talk to people," Becky says. Becky was shocked when she heard him address "Mom." "His mother died when he was three months old," Becky says, "so he never knew his mother."

"He kept saying 'I love you. I love you. I love you.' Over and over he would say that. And then he'd be watching, looking around. It was such an amazing thing," Becky says.

Becky woke up her family to let them know their father was now dying. Suddenly, the family heard a strange sound, like air moving quickly. "It was like the life was sucked out of him," Becky says. And then he died.

"Wow," Becky said, "He's gone from his body. We really are just vessels." The experience changed Becky's views of death and life after. "It gave me such great hope," she says with a smile. "After watching that, there is absolutely not a doubt in my mind that there is a heaven."

THE NORMALCY OF THE SUPERNATURAL

Being with those who are nearing death brings us nearer immortality, in the sense that those who are dying will soon be entering eternity. On the deathbed it is possible to have a preview of the next life. What's striking about the experiences of those near death is how natural the supernatural seems. Such intrusions are unexpected, perhaps, but not extraordinary. Though some people explain these occurrences as the physical result of the dying process, Christians throughout history and those who spend time with the dying today often believe there are spiritual explanations to seemingly spiritual events at the end of life.

We are used to the idea of the grim reaper from his appearances in fairy tales and horror flicks, but we don't much talk about real-life versions of such a visitor, whose visits to Paul and

Edward seem to have been welcomed rather than feared. Though our images of a deathbed visitor don't quite match what dying people appear to experience, there seems to be truth to the idea of a someone who comes to accompany a person at death. Dying people often report friendly visits (and, less frequently, hostile ones), sometimes from strangers, sometimes from friends and relatives. And usually these people have come to help them on their coming journey.

God works in many ways on the deathbed. Some people experience a sublime spiritual power as they bear witness to someone's death. Others experience a vivid encounter with the spiritual world as death draws close. And still others discover a renewed spiritual life following the diagnosis of a terminal disease but while they are still relatively healthy.

Nancy Capocy, a devout Christian and the director of a hospice program in suburban Chicago, has assisted hundreds of people in their deaths. She says the process of dying is as miraculous an event as being born. It is a basic physical event that is surrounded with mystery and miracle. Witnessing this process has "made my faith even stronger, as I see people making the transition."

Capocy says the presence of spiritual beings is often apparent. "As I'm watching people die, you can almost tell what they're seeing." Capocy says her patients often talk to or are aware of people unseen by everyone else.

Some people say these visions are hallucinations, the result of chemical changes in the dying brain. "I don't buy that," Capocy says. "I think they're talking to people who have died. And I don't think they're hallucinating. I think they actually see the people. I think they actually converse with them. I think people who have died before them are actually calling them home. And as I see that, it reaffirms my own my spiritual beliefs."

Rather than merely awaiting or dreading the terror of the grim reaper, death can be—in fact it is when we let it be—a spiritual journey as real as our salvation.

A nurse in Minnesota told me about the contrast between many of the deaths she witnesses in the intensive care unit of the hospital and the anticipated and prepared for death of her own grandmother. "I've seen just horrific deaths" in the hospital, Faith says. "The idea today is push and push and push and use technology until you can't anymore."

As a nurse, Faith believes in the work she does and the importance of the medical care she provides. Yet when it came to her grandmother who suffered from kidney failure, she said the most important decision they made was not to go to the hospital.

"My grandma was about eighty-six when she died. She had polio as a child, and lived very well with it." She was active as a young person, though the disease affected her. "She always kind of hobbled around." But when she was diagnosed with kidney failure, she decided not to have dialysis, in which a machine filters the toxins out of the blood. She said, "I don't want to have to go three to five days a week to sit in a chair for half a day to just be lethargic and tired and worn out at the end. I'm just going to putter along as I can in my house."

That's just what she did. Faith says she was the brains of the household and her grandfather was the brawn. "They worked well together for years." But eventually, Faith's grandmother had a couple of trips to the hospital within a short time, and she ended up in an assisted living home. It became clear through tests and continued health problems that her body was failing.

"Grandma was very realistic," Faith says. She told her family, "I'm not going to feel much better even if you do this or that. I've lived a good life. I've been blessed." They entered her in a hospice program where the nurses focused on minimizing the pain and providing other care. "The chaplain services were really supportive to the family," Faith says.

A few days before she died, Faith's grandmother told her family not to take her to the hospital when her blood pressure started to drop—an expected and recurring event because of her illness. Faith says that was the most important decision in what turned out to be a beautiful death. "You have to say I'm going to start dying, and you have to let me stay here to die. Otherwise she would have been rushed to the hospital and go through the admission and all of that again, and she'd been through that twice already. It just wasn't worth it."

As a result, Faith says, "She died in the nursing home with all of us there with her." The family and her grandmother would have preferred if she could have been at home, but it wasn't possible to remove her from the nursing home. So, the family decided to make her room their home by bringing in items from her house and visiting regularly.

"She really taught me how to live," Faith says, "and taught me how to die."

THE SPEAKER

While the moments when death occurs can be a deeply spiritual event, other times the prospect of dying brings about a spiritual renewal long before death actually arrives. In fact, when a terminal illness is seen as God's means of bringing about such a renewal, it can have profound consequences in the lives of numerous people outside the normal reach of that person's life. It shows that God can provide new meaning and hope, even in the life of someone whose days are numbered.

Jim Harrell was in the middle of a wonderful life when he received test confirmation that he had Lou Gehrig's disease, or ALS. Jim had always been a goof-off, a practical jokester, ready to find the humor in nearly everything, but at first it was hard to find anything funny about ALS. Jim ran his own consulting firm, where he advised clients on railroad labor relations. The eldest of his four children was in her teens, and Jim looked forward to seeing them off to college.

For a year, Jim said, he struggled with accepting the diagnosis. He was steadily losing the ability to use his muscles, so it wasn't a matter of acknowledging that he had the disease or facing up to the fact of it. That was obvious. "It was difficult to pray," Jim said, "and really mean 'Father, not my will but yours be done.' I didn't want to pray it and not mean it," Jim said. "But I didn't know how to pray it and mean it."

However, throughout that first year Jim did pray, especially with friends, seeking God's will. He read the books that had influenced him when he first became a Christian during college in Kansas, especially Francis Schaeffer and C. S. Lewis. And Jim was reading more of the Bible.

Jim said he'd always been involved with church, but he considered it church work. It didn't attract the focus and attention that his career had. But following his diagnosis Jim met with friends, and together they prayed for Jim and asked God for guidance during this final stage in Jim's life.

One friend of Jim's, a retired pastor who had been part of Jim's prayer group, asked him to speak to a group at the church the friend attended. The pastor asked Jim to talk about being a Christian in the business world. At the end of his messge, Jim said, he changed the topic and began talking about his disease. "I talked about the fact that I had this diagnosis and how much easier it had become for me to talk to non-Christians."

Jim's friend, the former pastor, was wrapping up the event, thanking Jim and reinforcing his message, when someone in the audience blurted out, "Wait, can we pray for Jim?" That moment was a turning point, Jim said. "First, it blew me away that people weren't falling asleep. But second, it was clear the Holy Spirit decided to use me."

Jim had never been one to enjoy standing in front of an audience. He was more of a Moses than an Aaron, he said, but Jim was invited to speak elsewhere. After a few more speaking engagements, he realized he received a similar response at each one. People were moved to hear him talk about how he was able to deal with his progressive illness with God's help. Each event, it seemed, God was using Jim's story to touch the hearts of anyone who heard it.

Still, it was only just dawning on Jim that God was giving him a mission for the last phase of his life. He was just considering spending more time speaking about his illness when he spoke at the annual staff meeting of a client. Jim spoke about railroad labor relations, but he then asked for a little more time. Jim told his story of getting ALS and how God had helped him deal with it.

It was, once again, a success, and with the help of friends, Jim started speaking to other non-Christian audiences too. His friends hired a company to produce a DVD so Jim wouldn't have to do all the speaking as his breathing worsened. And they arranged for speaking engagements. "It just sort of snowballed," he said.

At the same time, Jim's Bible suddenly took on a new life. "It was the Holy Spirit, I know, gripping me, because I had really turned around and viewed life differently," Jim said. "The big verse that hit me right between the eyes was 2 Corinthians 4:16-18."

Therefore we do not lose heart. Though outwardly we are wasting away, yet inwardly we are being renewed day by day. For our light and momentary troubles are achieving for us an eternal glory that far outweighs them all. So we fix our eyes not on what is seen, but on what is unseen. For what is seen is temporary, but what is unseen is eternal.

Jim says those verses overturned his perspective on his life and his illness. The speaking itself didn't change him, Jim said. "The speaking has given evidence of what the Holy Spirit's been doing in my life."

LETTING GO

Jim's renewed sense of purpose and spiritual vision came about with some difficulty. First, Jim said, he had to learn to trust that God would take care of his family. "I am a control guy," Jim explained. "It was unfathomable for me to figure out how God could take care of my wife and kids without me on the scene."

But reading Luke where Jesus talks about leaving family members behind for fidelity to Christ, Jim was struck by Jesus' words. It was exactly what he couldn't do. Jim said he heard God ask, "How much do you love me, Jim? Do you really love me enough to trust me to take care of your wife and your children?"

Once Jim had let go of his need to be his family's sole provider, his family had a surprise gift for him. Early on Easter Sunday morning, a friend came to get Jim and took him to church. The pastor met Jim outside, and the three friends walked through the church doors together. Inside, his pastor gave Jim a program for the event that was about to take place. His pastor said, "Jim, you have about a hundred friends in there, friends of yours, friends of your kids. Your wife has put this together. All four of your kids are going to get baptized."

That morning, Jim's kids all gave their testimonies and were baptized. "It was just a little service for our family and for our friends," Jim said. His wife also shared with their friends about the difficulties she had dealing with Jim's illness, but also the strength God had given her to handle her husband's death.

Jim wonders if his willingness to let God care for his family after his death had something to do with that Easter morning baptismal service. "I don't know," Jim says, but he has become a different man. Because of his experience of gradual dying, Jim has been given time to share his testimony, which has transformed others' lives. Now, says Jim, "I'm really ready to go home, and my family knows that. But I want to stay as long as I can." In addition, the opportunities to boldly witness to unbelievers and share fellowship with treasured friends have given Jim new perspective on life. "I don't know why I spent however many years of my adult life being nervous about sharing the gospel."

WHERE THE RUBBER MEETS THE ROAD

When Jim accepted that he was ready to be with the God he had come to love in a new way, his views of end-of-life care changed significantly. Among other things, Jim decided he would not artificially prolong his life with the help of medical technology. "I felt like if I can't breathe [naturally], then I'm ready to go." Jim admits it was a tough decision—one that his family didn't entirely agree with at first. But ALS, Jim says, doesn't attack the mind. Eventually, he would need a ventilator to breathe for him. But the rest of his body would still keep working until he couldn't move a muscle. "Pretty much you're completely, totally paralyzed, from the top of the head down." At that point, doctors decide to take the ventilator out. "I'm not afraid of death," Jim said, "but the dying part is still a little troublesome." Jim said he'd rather know and be ready for his death than to hear one day that doctors would remove his life support.

Jim had thought about those final moments in some detail. "I guess that in thirty seconds it would be over, but still it would be pretty awful for thirty seconds. And I don't think that I want to know that today's Tuesday, tomorrow's Wednesday and that's the day that we're going to pull the plug. I'd rather have God surprise me."

Until then, Jim says, "I've got goals," and he isn't ready to die. "Our youngest graduates from high school the first of June. Our twenty-fifth wedding anniversary is the end of July. I want to make that. But if I don't, that's okay." Still, he is willing for his life here on earth to end. His experience of gradual dying may take years, but Jim's affairs are in order now and his heart eagerly awaits its eternal home.

Jim quotes Joni Eareckson Tada, who says that God allows what he hates in order to accomplish what he loves. "I see how he's doing that in my life," Jim says. "If I had to do it all over again, I would absolutely choose ALS to get where I am spiritually versus not getting ALS and not being where I am spiritually."

Jim says ALS prompted him toward a renewed spiritual life. But he only realized what had been true throughout his life. "All our days are short," he says. "I'm living life with eternity right there. And I know that what I'm doing matters in eternity."

A SPIRITUAL REALITY

Those steps recommended by the Christian art of dying—expressing willingness to die, showing belief in Jesus, offering final thoughts and encouragements to family and friends, giving hope in the life to come—do more than create a peaceful and welcoming environment for the dying person. These actions prepare the spirit.

Repeated and intimate experience with the dying, over the course of centuries, taught Christians the necessary path to dying well. While everyone is different and these steps may not look alike from person to person, the general outline is the same. And Christian wisdom teaches that it works to bring a dying person on the right path from mortality to immortality.

It is typical today for many Christians to draw from the experiences of those who have, through some accident, experienced heaven while their bodies had died. Having neared death, such a person returns to life and shares with others those experiences of heaven. While these are often inspiring and faith-affirming accounts, such stories are not the typical experiences of dying people. Near-death experiences may teach us many things—such as offering proof that the body and person may exist independently. But these accounts don't necessarily offer the best proof of heaven or description of what it will be like. And they don't teach us to prepare ourselves or care for others who are dying. They don't teach us to die well.

However, the experiences of everyday Christians nearing their own deaths, combined with Scripture, can provide glimpses of heaven, details of the world to come and hope to attain to the place God has prepared for his children. These can offer us as Christians, congregations and caregivers an extra reason to hope in Christ's victory over death—and its implication for our own life to come.

6

THE HARDEST CONVERSATION
YOU'LL EVER HAVE

Today, it is almost impossible to die alone, as gradual dying often requires a group of caregivers to assist in the daily activities of life, like eating and bathing, and the tasks of medical care, such as trips to the doctor and the administration of medicine. It is amazing, therefore, that despite the entourage of people who must assemble to care for a dying person, we have so much difficulty bringing up the subject.

Conversations about our values and those of our loved ones at the end of life are certainly not easy. We are quick to believe that a family member's, or even our own, illness is not that bad. One woman told me that her brother sent her an email while their mother was in the intensive care unit in the hospital. He lived about an hour's drive away. Rather than offering to visit or any kind of support, he told her, "I don't think mom's really that sick." We all have our own personal obstacles to facing someone's death.

Even if we think that the time has come to have an end-of-life discussion, it can be nerve-wracking. We don't want people to think we are anticipating their deaths. And we don't want to force such an unpleasant subject on another person. Yet one of the most important things to do, in order to create an environment where a loved one can die well having complete relationships with family and friends, is to have this most difficult of conversations. The time for end-of-life discussions is long before they are ever needed. Then, when a health crisis comes, the conversation needs only to be updated and applied to a specific situation.

GETTING STARTED

Though a healthy, happy man, I felt it important to discuss my end-of-life desires with my wife. We had made reasonable preparations in case one of us died, such as making a will and taking out life-insurance policies. I had even discussed my end-of-life health care wishes.

However, I still worried that if I were to die suddenly within the next several years, I would leave my wife and children without a husband and father. I believe that eventually, no matter her claims to the contrary, she may want to remarry, and it was important to me to give her my blessing if she chose to do so. But it's not easy to tell someone you love deeply that she should feel free to remarry.

After a couple failed attempts, we talked about this difficult emotional component of our end-of-life wishes. We've had the conversation regarding if and when she might marry after I die, and she knows that I support any decision to remarry. I love her, and I know she will make wise decisions if I am no longer able to be at her side.

It was once that these situations were structured into social customs. If a husband died, his family took care of his wife and children. Deacons were charged with caring for widows and orphans. Yet today we have no more rituals, no manners to guide our behavior, no expectations to ease the path into these conversations. It is harder now that we have to start from scratch but nevertheless essential that we try. And the sooner and more often we discuss our end-of-life wishes (whether that end comes early or late in life) the better off we and our families will be. And the better our deaths will be.

HAVING A DISCUSSION

In such conversations, caregivers or potential caregivers should ask how someone would like to die. Hospital deaths and at-home deaths are different ways of dying, not just different locations. Someone who wants to have everything possible done to keep him alive will want to be where the most medical options are available, though it may limit time with family and spiritual activity. Someone whose ultimate wish is to die among family in a comfortable and familiar place will probably need to forgo some medical options. Learning this and other desires of parents, siblings and friends is often necessary for those who are terminally ill. It is a conversation between caregiver and patient, where each needs to be heard.

Caregivers cannot leave the conversation to others. Doctors are notoriously bad at it. "I've heard doctors say 'Do you want us to do everything possible for you if your heart were to stop or if you were to stop breathing?'" says David Fisher, a hospice doctor who began practicing end-of-life care after frequently seeing it badly done. "Well of course the family would say they want you to do everything possible. That's not the way to ask the question."

A January 2010 study published in the journal *Cancer* confirms Fisher's analysis. The survey of four thousand doctors found that just one quarter would be willing to discuss hospice or the pa-

tient's preferred site of death when the patient was judged to
have four to six months to live. The doctors said they would
rather begin those discussions once there were no more treatments to offer. This is despite guidelines that ask doctors to talk
with patients about these issues when they still have a full year of
life left.[1]

People want to be cared for, even if they don't want every possible procedure performed on them. The way to ask the question, Fisher says, is "Do you want us to pound on your chest, put
a tube in, put you on a machine even if it's not likely to benefit
you?" That's what "everything possible" means in practical terms.
These kinds of interventions may add some time to someone's
life, perhaps a day or more depending on the situation. But,
Fisher says, when patients understand that so-called heroic measures performed on the terminally ill rarely add value to a life
even if they extend it, they'd typically rather have peace.

"I saw a lot of patients and families who were dealing with a
terminal illness," Fisher told me on a bench outside a nursing
home where many of his patients live on the shore of Lake Mich-
igan on Chicago's South side. "A lot of times, they seemed confused about how to approach it, and what they were allowed to
do, what they were obligated to do."

Unfortunately, doctors were typically of little help, Fisher says.
With no training in how to discuss end-of-life issues with patients
or families, doctors often avoided these difficult moments. When
it could no longer be postponed and doctors needed to know what
to do should a patient's heart or breathing stop, it was often too
late for the conversation to be of much good, Fisher says.

"I saw a need to try to perfect my own skills discussing end-
of-life issues with people," Fisher says. "I felt like I was doing a
real service to patients and families to talk about these issues

long before you're actually at the crux of the decision making."

"The ICU is a bad place to have an end-of-life care discussion," Fisher says. Aside from the trauma of having a loved one in intensive care, the patient is usually unable to even speak for him- or herself.

Fisher has learned a few things that he recommends to others who are having such a conversation, whether with someone who is very ill or quite healthy. "I always try to frame my discussions around goals of care," Fisher says. "That helps people better frame their decisions. If their goal is to live as long as possible, trying every treatment available, then we'll do that. But if a patient's goal is to not be in pain, or not suffer, or stay at home, or see a grand-daughter graduate, then we can work toward that."

If possible, it is important to have these conversations outside the hospital. As an intensive care nurse, Faith Zwirchitz has seen both beautiful deaths and horrific ones. "You get a false hope" from technology, she says. "You get to a point where families don't realize where they're at medically," because all the intervention hides the true extent of the illness. As a result, "It's harder to withdraw the ventilator or the dialysis," she says. "It's harder to withdraw those cares than to put the patient on it. So I think a big thing that contributes to a good end of life is communication." Unless a family knows they want something else, the direction modern health care leans is toward more technology and intervention. Faith says, often simply for fear of a lawsuit. "You can keep people alive for quite some time on machines," Faith says. And once the technology has started, it's tough to remove.

Faith says families that have talked things over, who know what they want out of the end of life, tend to experience good deaths. "Have an ongoing conversation throughout life," Faith says, "from the time you're young to who knows when death is going to come. When families have spoken with their loved ones, or when friends have spoken with loved ones and said, This is how I want my life to be lived; this is how I wouldn't, that's really helpful."

WHAT TO ASK

In his essay "I Want to Burden My Loved Ones," Gilbert Meilaender gently argues against the application of living wills or advance directives as the modern fix-all to the tendency of doctors to rely too heavily on medicine. We say we don't want to burden our families with making difficult choices when we cannot make medical decisions on our own, so we turn to legal documents that outline what we would and would not want should we ever be unable to tell a doctor ourselves.

But Meilaender, a professor of theology at Valparaiso University and member of former President George W. Bush's Council on Bioethics, says that this appeal to a piece of paper overturns what families are supposed to do—carry each other's burdens. When we allow someone else to care for us, make decisions for us, Meilaender says, we most often discover that they are willing and eager to pick up our burdens.

"It is, therefore, essential," Meilaender writes, "that we structure the medical decision-making situation in such a way that conversation is forced among the doctor, the medical caregivers, the patient's family, and perhaps still others, such as a pastor."[2]

Meilaender says that advance directives are not bad or wrong. But it is best when a range of people—family, doctors, pastors and someone appointed by the patient with legal authority to make decisions—are a part of the conversation about what medical care a patient desires. When an advance directive helps get these conversations started, it can go a long way toward directing a patient's medical care, because patients and families need to talk about these tough issues. That is the main benefit. Having a legal document in support of the patient's expressed wishes that can be used to ensure those wishes are acted on is a side benefit.

When a possibly terminal disease has already been diagnosed, it can be helpful to guide the conversation around the possible outcomes. John Dunlop, a gerontologist, says there are several questions to ask doctors about a terminal illness.

- What is the exact diagnosis? Learn all you can about the disease and how it will affect someone who suffers from it.

- What is the natural prognosis of the condition without treatment? If you were to allow the disease to advance, what would happen? Some diseases are less painful than others, some may allow life to continue normally for some time. Curative treatment might be more arduous than the natural progression of the disease.

- What are the treatment options for the disease? What are the chances for success? Some treatments are more painful than others; some may be worse than the actual disease. Chemotherapy is often one such treatment. It requires tremendous amounts of energy to endure and recover from, and depending on the potential outcome may be worse than simply letting the disease run its course. On the other hand, chemotherapy is quite effective in fighting cancer, so the benefits and risks must be weighed.

- What are the potential complications of the treatment under consideration? Some treatments are more likely than others to put families in ethical dilemmas. Alzheimer's patients may need a feeding tube because they sometimes refuse to eat. It helps to discuss beforehand under what conditions a patient or family would want a feeding tube inserted and removed. Feeding an otherwise healthy person who simply will not or cannot eat is different than artificially feeding a dying person. A feeding tube can painfully prolong dying as the body requires energy to digest the food at a time when it needs to focus on shutting down organs. Answering such questions based on a diagnosis in advance, or even just thinking about them, eases the decision making process when the time comes.[3]

Whatever treatment choices are made, Christians can value life by working with doctors to prolong it or make it more comfortable—and possibly richer—though shorter. One patient with terminal cancer told me that he intentionally stays engaged with coworkers, academic publishing schedules and family life in order to avoid the inward focus he had observed in many people before they died. Or Christians may value life by recognizing God's call to heaven. John Dunlop says he observes a slow detachment from life in his elderly patients. Eventually, it's time to go. Either way, by thoughtfully engaging how a patient's values will influence her medical decisions, families can offer better support. Even when a family member disagrees with a patient's choices, understanding why someone chooses a hospital setting rather than home, or vice versa, helps family members to be supportive and to be able to grieve when that person dies.

A patient's readiness to die translates into what care he or she wants. Because these values are very personal and can change as a patient feels that death approaches, families must be in conversation. Often family members have to implement a dying person's wishes. "Living wills," like the Five Wishes, simply give legal enforcement (and therefore a guarantee to the hospital that it will not be sued) to a patient's desires. However, they can always be changed or rejected entirely (simply by throwing it out).

But the point is not to pin down what doctors should or should not do in any unforeseeable circumstance. It is to provide an opportunity for families to discuss a patient's medical desires. Because our views may change, because we cannot know what medical options may be relevant, or what their ethical or relational implications may be, our conversations should simply reflect our values: this is what I want my last days to look like.

7

CARING FOR THE DYING

Katharine Jefferson had always been close to her brother. They grew up in Chicago, where Katharine eventually settled with her husband, Paul. Though Katharine's brother, Bob, and his wife, Cindy, began their family in Little Rock, Arkansas, the two couples regularly kept in touch. Katharine, everybody said, was the female version of Bob. The siblings were not only alike in their personality, they were close friends.

In fall 2004, Katharine and Paul were planning their retirement to a small town in Tennessee. The Jeffersons had purchased a plot of land in the hills along a river where they would enjoy the warmer Southern weather.

That autumn, Katharine's brother was just one step ahead of her. He and Cindy were moving into their retirement home in Melbourne, Florida, south of Cape Canaveral. Bob had been feeling unwell for a few months. He was losing weight and complained of ulcers, but too busy with the move, he didn't see a doctor. Ignoring his worsening health gave the family space to deal with one issue at a time. They moved into their new house during the deadly hurricane season of that year. Hurricanes

Charley, Frances, Ivan and Jeannie all slammed into the Florida
coast during August and September. It was during one of these
storms that Bob could no longer delay seeing the doctor.

Amid the destruction of the hurricane, Cindy took Bob to the
emergency room. In the hallway of the hospital, alongside victims of the storm, he wondered what storm was lashing his own
body. And why now, just as he and Cindy were beginning their
retirement?

WHAT ABOUT BOB?

Bob had always been a friendly and outgoing guy. He was a run-
ner and had been in good health. By the time he died of pancre-
atic cancer two years after his visit to the emergency room, he
had campaigned for Melbourne's mayor, the town he had just
moved to. He became friends with the mail carrier and the gar-
bage collector. "Who makes friends while they're dying?" Katharine's husband asked. But Bob did, and his funeral was packed.

When he called his family with news that he had developed
cancer, it was a shock. "Once someone has cancer, all your conversations are about that," Katharine said. Characteristically,
Bob was upbeat and positive about his prognosis. And at first, it
looked promising. Though he had delayed seeing the doctor, the
cancer was still early enough in its development for Bob to qual-
ify for the Whipple Procedure, in which surgeons remove parts
of the pancreas, small intestines and other organs. He found a
nearby hospital where he could have the surgery, and the doctors' reports afterward were encouraging. They had removed all
the cancer, he told Katharine.

Following the operation Katharine spent a week in Florida
helping to take care of her brother and his family while he recovered from the procedure and began chemotherapy. "It was rough

on him," Katharine said. "He had a hard time in the hospital," and then when he arrived home and recovered, Bob began chemo. Finally, by the beginning of 2005, it looked as though he had simply been through a terrible scare. For the next nine months, doctors continued to keep an eye on the cancer, and Bob finally began the retirement he had hoped to start the previous fall.

But in late 2005, doctors discovered that the cancer had returned, this time in the liver and other organs. Surgery was out of the question because the cancer had encompassed nearly all of the liver. Doctors began aggressive chemotherapy, and Bob suffered terribly. This time, nothing the doctors did stopped the cancer.

By 2006 he was very sick, but he decided to try experimental treatments in Delaware. Because they couldn't afford for him and his wife to go, Bob made many of the trips alone. But the therapy proved ineffective, and in November 2006, he decided he was too exhausted to continue.

Having decided not to pursue further treatment, Bob called his sister. "I think this is it," he told Katharine. "I don't want to let anybody down, but I can't do this anymore." He was afraid of dying in the hospital alone a thousand miles from his wife in Florida and his daughters in Arkansas. Bob said he wanted to have peace during the time he had left, and he wanted to spend it with the people he cared about. At first, his family wasn't convinced he'd made the right decision, and they looked for other medical options. Though some experimental procedures were available, they eventually decided not to pursue them. "You're not letting anybody down," Katharine told her brother. "We support you in whatever you decide." Cindy, Bob's wife, called hospice and his six siblings, telling them if they wanted to see Bob before he died, they should visit soon.

Katharine and Paul made plans to head to Florida and stay with Bob until he died. "I just felt that I had to be there when he died," Katharine said. Thirty years ago Katharine's mother had died in the hospital. Nurses discovered her fallen on the floor. Katharine not only felt terrible for not being there for her mother, she was also saddened to have missed an opportunity to spend invaluable time with her. "There wasn't hospice then," Katharine said. Her dad had also died while Katharine was away, and she didn't want to lose this chance to be with her brother. The day they arrived, Katharine and Paul chatted with Bob while he was awake. But "that was the last clear conversation we had," Paul said. "He just slid right down after that."

Other family members arrived as well. Of Bob's six brothers and sisters, three siblings and two in-laws along with two of his three daughters came to be with him while he died. One sister, a nurse, showed Katharine and Cindy how to make the bed while Bob was in it. Together they fumbled through changing sheets while he lay in his hospital bed. Katharine stepped in to help with caring for her brother. "We'd get up at night to change his bedsheets and his diapers," she said. "That was hard for him," she said. "Part of our journey is learning to let people care for us in that way." Bob once asked Katharine how she could do it. "Because I love you," she said. "I do this because you'd do it for me."

"You're just learning," Katharine said. "There's no place to go to school for this, but you learn as you go." Bob's daughters came from Little Rock, and they pitched in by shifting him in the bed to prevent bedsores. Paul and Katharine stayed with a neighbor to make room in Bob's house as more people arrived.

Bob kept up his spirits. "He loved life," Katharine said, "and he was going to enjoy it till it was over." He continued to play the central role in the family that he always had, by interjecting himself unexpectedly into conversations when others thought he was sleeping.

Bob and Katharine's father, who had watched his own brother die, had frequently said a person should never watch a sibling die. "I think that was in the back of Bob's mind," Katharine said. On the day he died, the members of the family who had gathered to be with him at his death assembled in the living room. Bob lay on his hospital bed while the family told stories of their childhood and sang songs. Katharine felt that he needed to be alone, and she asked Cindy if they should leave the room for a while. Cindy then asked Bob if they should leave, and he nodded.

"I'll go make cocktails," Cindy said. "And don't you worry," she told Bob, who was particular about how he made drinks for company. "I know how to make a cocktail!" The family crowded in the kitchen for drinks, and after a little while Cindy went to check on her husband.

Bob was dying, and Cindy asked everyone to gather next to him. He was ready to go. "He just caved in," Katharine said as he took his last breath. "Everything gets sucked out." Suddenly, he was no longer Bob. "You could see how God had breathed his life into you, and how it left. Then I knew he had died."

Earlier that day, Katharine had told Bob it was all right for him to go. "The Lord has a plan," she said. "You don't need to be afraid. Just relax and go." They had a short but meaningful conversation that day. As siblings, Katharine says, "We were of the same cloth."

JOURNEYING TO WHAT?

Bob's dying process lasted more than two years after he was diagnosed with cancer. While gradual dying can strain family resources as members care for an ill person or struggle to pay medical bills, it also provides opportunities for families to care for each other. This can be particularly meaningful when it is the last time we will be able to care for someone we love.

Caregiving for a dying person is full-time work. It can be exhausting, even for someone like Cindy, who was healthy, able, retired and had plenty of help from friends and family. On top of the physical effort, a terminal illness requires navigating the complex health-care system of insurance, medicine and doctors. Patients take trips to the hospital, undergo surgery perhaps, and need time to recover. All this goes on in addition to the mundane requirements of life—meals, children's soccer games, lawn mowing.

But a good death requires more than car rides and spoon feeding. Relationships need completing and sometimes mending. Faith needs nurturing. Often, stories need telling. There is no program for this kind of end-of-life work. Nevertheless, learning to give care, whether over months and years, or on occasional weekends, helps to smooth the path toward a good death.

There is indeed work to be done, perhaps the most important work—the work of completing a life. A dying person may set goals to fulfill, such as writing a life story or working on another kind of life review. A milestone, an anniversary, the birth of a grandchild or a daughter's wedding might become a courage-inspiring goal. People need to say goodbye to family and friends. And, importantly, they need to ready themselves spiritually. This is a different sort of journey, but it still takes time and effort. For caregivers, it is these tasks that, while adding to responsibilities, are the meaningful ones.

So, how do we actually do all these things? How do we care for a dying person? How do we honor their last days as significant? How do we make meaningful visits to someone terminally ill? Despite all the difficulty, all the awkwardness, all the pain, the answer is quite simple. Be present. However, if it is a simple answer, it is not an easy one to practice.

A CHRISTIAN TRADITION OF CARE

The Old Testament taught, and early Christians inherited, a belief in the unity of the body and spirit, and the sacredness of the body, created in the image of God. "It was to save the body that Christ took on flesh in the Incarnation," writes Gary B. Ferngren in *Medicine and Health Care in Early Christianity*.[1] This sense of the sacredness of the body and its unity with the soul meant that Christians saw the diseased body in a very different light. Unlike their pagan neighbors, who saw the soul as eternal and the body as dispensable, Christians could not abandon the ill, the dying and the dead.

This theological belief gave impetus to an amazing and effective health care system. "The local congregation created in the first two centuries of its existence an organization, unique in the classical world, that effectively and systematically cared for its sick."[2] By the year 251, the church in Rome supported fifteen hundred widows and sick members. In the fourth century, Antioch had three thousand people on the rolls of those receiving care from the church. From these early efforts came the first hospitals, dedicating to caring for the sick. Sociologist Rodney Stark argues that these efforts meant that Christians had a lower death rate and more readily converted outsiders, which is a major reason for the early church's rapid rate of growth.

While our society has forgotten its deathbed manners, as Christians we have a wealth of useful habits gathered through churchgoing: public prayer, singing, care for the needy, testimonies, shared food and a common belief about the meaning of life and death. These habits help us today just as they helped our earliest Christian brothers and sisters.

OVERCOMING OUR APPREHENSIONS

As we seek to be present with the dying and care for them in practical ways, we must overcome apprehensions that keep us from actively engaging in the life of the individual. We may fear that a visit itself, or what we might say during it, signals that we think death is near. We fear that acknowledging death's nearness would be offensive or at least unwelcome to whoever is ill. We may have our own dislike of being in a hospital. We may feel guilty for not visiting a loved one more often when she was healthy. Now that she's ill we feel awkward about making sudden and frequent visits.

Yet the most important thing to do is to be with someone facing death. It can bring families together, and it can be a healthy reminder that no matter how much we'd rather not think about it, none of us will be around very much longer. And in the end it will help our loved ones die more peacefully; it will help us grieve more easily.[3]

In truth, dying people are often "not so much afraid of death as they are of the process of dying. They fear progressive isolation, and they fear being forced to go it alone."[4] Being present also means coming to terms with the fact that someone you love is dying. Holding out hope for a person's recovery can be a way of isolating yourself from him or her.[5] And we may have apprehensions about attending the bedside when death is near, because dying patients often narrow down their circle of relationships due to increasing weariness.

Caring for a dying person presents a range of challenges for the caregiver, but not because each individual task is difficult. As loved ones are able to put to rest their apprehensions, they will be able to engage more fully in loving the dying patient to the very end. We often say "there is nothing left to do" when medical options to cure an illness run out. But there is so much left to be done. As family members we can offer hope—not in extended life but in the goodness, purposefulness and blessedness of life. In addition to volunteering practical help, we can tell stories, sing songs, read Scripture and pray. For "much of what the dying and their families need can be given by non-professionals, caring friends, and churches," says nurse Arlene Miller. "Meals, notes, funny stories, quiet presence, respite care: all are ways to say, 'We care.'"[6]

BEING PRESENT

We live in an impossibly busy society. Our economy forces us to be transient people as jobs, or the pursuit of good ones, often require us to live great distances from the people we love. Maintaining long-term relationships is already difficult. No matter how much we love and care for a person, often it is simply too easy to neglect the work that relationships require. Then, when a loved one receives the diagnosis of a terminal illness, our discomfort with dying puts up an additional barrier to achieving completeness in a relationship that will soon end. Even when our relationships are healthy, the pain of loss can be too much to bear. When relationships are strained, it can be painfully difficult to talk about a terminal illness or say the necessary words.

For some time after my Aunt Eileen died, I wondered what I should have done, how I should have behaved as my aunt lay dying in her bedroom. The director of the local hospice program relieved my concern when she told me there was no need to feel guilty for not knowing what to do.

"You had visited her," Nancy Capocy told me, "and you went there when she was dying and you just stood there. But you did it. Your presence is what you needed to do. The fact that you went there. Sometimes there isn't anything to do, any task to do. Sometimes our presence is doing more than anything else that could be done. Presence," she said, "is a very powerful, powerful thing."

Our busy lives and the added work of caring for a dying person make it difficult. Our fear of dying creates discomfort being with someone facing such difficult circumstances. All these obstacles make it difficult, even when we are able to visit, to have a meaningful presence with someone on his or her deathbed. Yet Dallas Willard, author of *The Divine Conspiracy* and several other books on spiritual formation, says that it is no small thing to be truly present with someone. "What we want to do is to carry with us at all times a consciousness that we are spiritual beings with an eternal destiny in God's universe," Willard told me. This consciousness, or walking in the Spirit, as the New Testament says, gives us a peacefulness wherever we are, whatever we are doing.

This spiritual sensitivity is important as we spend time with those who are making a transition of spirit. "When we deal with people who are on the verge of death, or their loved ones," says Willard, who has also worked as a pastor, "we want to bring that same spirit of peace into their lives." Sometimes you can't say much. But a spiritual presence, he says, can help a person come to grips with what is happening to them. "I think that reassures them of the substantiality of their soul, to put it in grandiose language," Willard says. "They are received, and that makes a difference."

"The spirit of peace and joy that you carry in yourself, you can extend that to them." This presence, Willard says, is not a formula. It is not a matter of saying certain words. "We really need to understand what it is like to be with a person and not have to manage that," he says, "how to look into their eyes and listen to them."

"That's the greatest blessing you can give to people, to be with them in those kinds of situations and to avoid the temptation to try to explain it or smooth it out. Just let it be," Willard counsels, "be with them."

This sort of caregiving, the care of spiritual presence, comes from family or others who have a personal relationship with the dying person. In the typical hospital or medical situation, say hospice nurses Maggie Callanan and Patricia Kelly, "relatives and friends become spectators watching something occur—not in a continuous stream of emotions and experiences from which to learn, but in awkward chunks of time."[7] Whether dying occurs in a hospital bed or at home, as spiritual caregivers we must be ready to use those opportunities.

COMPLETING LIFE

The biggest factor that makes for good deaths, says hospice doctor Ira Byock, is family relationships. In his experience, "Patients who died most peacefully and families who felt enriched by the passing of a loved one tended to be particularly active in terms of their relationships and discussions of personal and spiritual matters. These families in particular also seemed to be involved in the person's physical care. In the broadest sense, it was as if dying from a progressive illness had provided them with opportunities to resolve and complete their relationships and to get their affairs in order."[8]

Even in those situations where death does not come gradually, thinking about our death encourages us to live in such a way that our relationships don't need special time to complete, that our spiritual life is progressing and our need for apologies and forgiveness are up to date.

As we learn to be present with the dying, we can go on to make sure our relationships are complete. We must mend, strengthen and celebrate our relationships with those we love. Byock says we all need to say four things to a dying person: "Please forgive me," "I forgive you," "Thank you" and "I love you."

Though Byock does not write as a Christian, these words have ample biblical precedent. Isaac blessed Jacob before his death. Jacob blessed his children after he finally reached Egypt and his family was reunited. Stephen asked for forgiveness on behalf of his murderers. Jesus asked John to take care of his mother.

These words are deeply human. Paul Jefferson told me that on the day his brother-in-law died he felt the need to bless him. Putting his hand on Bob and saying a prayer, he did bless Bob, though it felt a bit awkward and Paul wasn't quite sure why he felt he should. Yet Paul was doing only what faithful believers have done for thousands of years.

Marge Schaffer, a nursing professor at Bethel University in the Twin Cities, has studied dying, both academically and as a Christian nurse. Dying well, she says, means being at peace with God and with the people in your life. "That's a very important part of dying, that one could say 'I've said what I needed. I made peace in my relationships.'"

"A 'good' death," says hospice nurse Martha Twaddle, "is most often as important for friends and families as for the dying patient. The witnessed death experience becomes a living memory for the survivors; a comfortable death can often facilitate closure for a grieving family."[9] In this way a dying person is able to complete his or her relationships on earth, and caregivers are able to complete their relationships with a loved one.

SPIRITUALLY COMPLETE

For Christians, complete relationships include a spiritual element. Caregivers can encourage a dying person's spiritual life with God. Al Weir is the president for campus and community ministries at the Christian Medical and Dental Association. As an oncologist he has often seen patients die well. But he also has seen Christians who did not die well. "Some people just have a culture or an environment or a personality or people around them that make it difficult for them to die," he told me. "Others are well supported or have been raised in such a way that they understand. It varies tremendously even from Christian to Christian."

Curious about these differences, Weir, the author of *When Your Doctor Has Bad News: Simple Steps to Strength, Healing, and Hope,* wanted to determine what made the difference. "Is it a matter of faith?" he asked. "Is it those who spend more time in church or those who pray better or those who seem more faithful to the Lord?"

But Weir found that dying well wasn't determined by visible spiritual practice. "There are very faithful people who've died in fright," he told me. "I don't think there's a magic formula. As I look back over my career, those who were confident in their relationship with the Lord, those who were confident that God was with them, and those who had family members that also felt the same way, they tended to be the ones that died well."

"It was a real and ongoing relationship [with God]," Weir says. "It was not necessarily connected to faith practices—did they pray, did they believe God was going to heal them, did they go to church. Those kinds of things weren't necessarily connected." Instead, Weir says, a spiritual relationship with God alongside belief that following death they would be with those who loved and cared for them in this life were the biggest factors in achieving a good death.

Learning to be spiritually present with people not only overcomes the deficiencies of the modern hospital and our own frantic lives, it also allows us to finish our relationships with those we care for.

OVERCOMING THE CHALLENGES OF MEDICINE

Hospice nurses Callanan and Kelley liken their work to the work of midwives.[10] Instead of birthing babies, they birth souls. Of course, they are not the first to compare the travail of dying to that of birth. Martin Luther, John Donne and Christians throughout the centuries made the same comparison. And in death, just as in birth, medical considerations are both central and peripheral. The miracle of birth is not in the fact that doctors and nurses ensure the safety of mother and child. The miracle of a good death is aided by good medical care, but not dependent on it.

The gift a good death gives to family and friends is similar. Dying well is not a medical event. For centuries Christians have practiced the art of dying without the major medical intervention available today. Yet modern doctors and nurses can assist and even provide opportunities for a good death. Hospice is a good example but certainly not the only one.

Medicine can also turn death into a nightmare, as anyone can attest who has agonized while a loved one was kept alive with machines and IVs. With the vision of what a good death looks like, those who are caring for a dying loved one can help make medical decisions that allow for a that person to die in peace and hope. It is through conversations, medical choices that align with our values, and a personal presence that helps us care, in difficult circumstances, for those we love.

Having end-of-life conversations, making wise choices toward a good death and being present with dying loved ones are especially important because our medical system is not designed to help people die. Despite the remarkable advances of modern medicine, which have led to longer lives, journalist Virginia Morris says that doctors and hospitals often make the difficult work of dying even more arduous. Often hospitals are an obstacle to a good death, simply because they're not in the business of helping people to die but to live. This is not a condemnation of the medical system, which does an excellent job healing the sick. But it is simply not arranged and its workers are not trained to help people make wise end-of-life choices.

Too often patients and families have suffered as someone endured what would turn out to be the futile life-saving efforts so quickly employed by hospitals. Our culture's feared image of death is not a swift one or a lonely one but a medicalized one, in which a patient is kept alive by machines and can only die if they are "unplugged." In response, Americans have urged the even more unfortunate alternative of assisted suicide. Hospitalized dying has become so terrible that a few people would rather doctors help them kill themselves.

The challenge for patients and their families is to know when to stop. There often comes a time when doctors, families and patients need to prepare themselves for death. And they need to know when to forego medical treatment intended to cure and turn instead to treatment that promotes comfort.

Since there is always something else that a doctor can do, patients and their families need to know, as Bob did, when it is no longer time to seek a cure and instead seek a peaceful end. Even if this occurs in a hospital, it is an important part of the Christian tradition of dying well for a dying person to achieve that willingness to die.

CAREGIVING ALONE AND MAKING FAMILY DECISIONS

Caring for a loved one who is dying becomes immensely more difficult and frustrating when only one family member has been doing the caregiving. Often only that person is able to recognize the nearness of death. The person most involved in caregiving is able to see that a loved one's health problems are not just a series of one-time, isolated health problems. Rather they are symptoms of deeper problems, that he is dying.

When Grandpa, for example, is having trouble getting enough to eat and is sometimes confused, a fall may send him to the emergency room. Months later, he returns due to shortness of breath. Then, shortly after, a strange pain appears that make doctors want to perform a series of potentially invasive and expensive tests. You may recognize that all these different problems have a single underlying cause: old age leading to death. But family members, out of love for Grandpa, but perhaps without a complete picture of the situation, may disagree. All Grandpa needs, they say, is some attention from doctors.

These are difficult issues. Grandpa may recover and live healthily for several more years. He may only partially respond to treatment and live longer but suffer extensively. Or he may not pursue curative treatment and enter a palliative program that offers comfort, which leads to better mental well-being, which in turn leads to a couple years of enjoyable life. Grandpa's health problems may indicate something much more serious, and he may only live a few more weeks. One hospice worker told me her first three patients all recovered; she was still waiting for one to die. How do we provide care in such a complex environment?

One doctor told me of a patient who, along with her husband, had decided to enter hospice. The doctor then began talking with the couple not only about her medical options but also about how she would use her remaining time. "If we're not going to fight this," he told them, "what do you need to do between now and then? One, you need to spend the time with family. Second," he asked, "do you know you're going to heaven?" Depending on his relationship with patients and their relationship with God, this doctor tries to nudge, in respectful and appropriate ways, his patients' thoughts toward eternity.

"This way," the doctor, who has a private practice, told me, "she's dying in a way that is reflective. She's thinking it through, as much as she's able to think. But certainly her husband will be much more prepared with the groundwork we laid than if we had put her in the hospital."

He was doing his best to help her die well and, to the extent possible, prepare for eternity. He knew the couple well, and with years of experience he understood the challenges they faced. But he couldn't as easily have the same discussion with the couple's children. Following the decision to enter hospice, the doctor received phone calls from both children, who asked why more wasn't being done. Plenty was being done for the woman, of course. She was loved and cared for, and she received regular visits from her doctor. But she was not getting aggressive medical treatment intended to cure. For those family members far away, it was hard to understand, and they were not going to easily accept their mother's entrance into a hospice program.

So, what do we do? How do single caregivers tell the rest of the family that Grandpa has confided in us when other family members have expressed deep concern about making the choices Grandpa has asked to be made? If Grandpa is mentally confused, how do we explain that we know his wishes best, having cared for him over the last few years? What if, on the other hand, we're convinced that it's worth giving doctors a chance to provide long-term health, even if it means short-term suffering through tests or medical procedures?

There is no formula to reach an answer to these difficult questions. And an inability to resolve them can lead to years of family conflict. On the other hand, wrestling through these issues as a family can bring a family together in the most meaningful way. One pastor tells me that these circumstances always expose the brokenness in our relationships. These are opportunities for Jesus to draw all the members of a family closer to himself, he says. But only if we allow it.

Caregivers may have the most insight into the best answers, but they may not recognize that others need time to come to terms with their own concerns and discover what is best. There are certainly right and wrong choices here—euthanasia, for example, or an insistence on extending life at all costs. But for the most part, the options before a family are choices between hard and harder. There is no joyful, easy road through the "valley of the shadow of death." In these circumstances families are seeking the best way to navigate difficult and dark terrain. What is needed is patience, time and an abundance of understanding. We must acknowledge that the best options may never be known.

Conflict may best be addressed by spending time together and especially with the ill loved one. A brother who lives far away or is too busy to visit may simply need time with Grandpa. But he will have to recognize his need on his own. And there may be very personal and deep issues that make this realization difficult to accept.

Compassion and understanding, time and prayer may be the best options for any family struggling to answer these questions. What's important is that families seek answers together and, as the Jefferson family did, offer care and assistance together.

In addition to family disagreements, the person most involved in caring for someone dying, whether husband or wife, son or daughter, may feel a desire for the end to come or feel a sense of relief when it does. This combination of grief and guilt is natural. Long-term caregiving is hard and often thankless work. It is not wrong to feel relieved of the task. It is holy work that includes modern-day caregivers in a long line of Christians dedicated to the care of the sick and dying, a tradition that reaches back to the earliest churches.

LUNCH ON THE DECK

Whether we struggle to accept our loved one's terminal diagnosis or we feel squeamish about interacting so physically with a dying person, our presence is the most powerful measure of care we can offer. If we're not sure where to start, creating the conditions for a good death can sometimes be as simple as having lunch on the deck.

Nancy Capocy, a director at the local hospice, had a patient with an open wound down her stomach following surgery in the hospital. Margaret was confined to her bed. Her husband couldn't get around well and needed two canes.

Her husband, Paul, had a deck built for her for when she came home. Unfortunately, she never recovered as he anticipated, and being bedridden, Margaret had not yet gotten to see the deck outside her own back door. "One of my greatest disappointments in life," she told Nancy, "is that I'll never get to see that deck."

Nancy responded, "You don't say that to a hospice nurse." She asked Paul if they had a wheelchair. One was in the garage, so Nancy cleaned it up and called other nurses for some help.

"We took her out of bed, put her in that wheelchair, and took her out on her deck," Nancy says. "She was so happy. She sat out there for a while, but she started hurting." Margaret decided she'd better head back inside. "It's time for my morphine, and I need to eat," she said. "But this is the most glorious thing." Instead, Capocy brought her medicine and lunch outside. "All of her neighbors came, and they took pictures." The friends talked and told stories, ate and waited for the evening to settle in.

She died soon after. "Right before she died," Nancy says, "she told me, 'I always showed my family how to live. Now I'm going to show them how to die.'"

"I was standing by her bed when she died, and she was still alert enough to talk. Her husband was sitting on the other side of the bed, and he was sobbing. She looked over at him, and she said 'Paul, please don't cry.'"

"I knew he couldn't help crying. He loved her so much. And I kind of leaned down and whispered in her ear. 'You know, Margaret, if I was in your place and my husband was sitting beside my bed, he better be crying.'"

She turned around and looked at him, and she said, "Cry, Paul."

He now had his wife's understanding and permission to do what he needed to. Margaret died a few hours later. "It was a beautiful experience," Capocy says. "She was a good Christian. She knew what was going to happen to her after she died. And she was not afraid."

Learning to be with a dying person and create an environment in which he or she can complete relationships with loved one does not come automatically. Our own inabilities and discomfort can pose obstacles to saying the things we need to say, offering forgiveness and expressing love to those we love. These apprehensions can make it difficult for caregivers to have the end-of-life conversations that our medical system often makes necessary if we are to help loved ones make choices that assist in their dying well.

Yet all these difficulties and obstacles can be overcome by one simple thing: our presence. Even when we fail to do this or that task or say the right thing, being present makes up for our inadequacies and allows relationships to heal, grow and become complete.

8

THE CHRISTIAN FUNERAL

WHAT WE DO AND WHAT WE SAY WHEN SOMEONE dies is an expression of what we believe about life and how we want to live. The altars people create following the death of a movie celebrity or pop singer reveal who our culture worships. When people say that someone will live on in our hearts, they express their faith in a specific eternal destination.

But not all expressions at death are filled with pop-culture sentimentality. At the funeral of a long-time naval officer, I saw how our country, particularly our armed forces, views death. The funeral was a Christian service, presided over by the deceased's thoughtful and well-spoken pastor. But while his Christian faith was the most important aspect of the man's life, he also spent a number of years in full-time and reserved naval service.

During the graveside service, a handful of naval officers were present to offer thanks and pay their respects to a man who had served his country. First bugles saluted the soldier. A flag draped the coffin, and two soldiers picked it up, and with military discipline, folded it. They handed the flag to their superior officer, who then took it to the soldier's widow. The officer spoke loudly and clearly of the honorable service her husband gave and of the country's deep appreciation. He handed the flag to the widow, took her hand and kissed her cheek. He then offered condolences one by one to every member of the family.

Watching this, it struck me how solemnly the military considers the death of a service man or woman. Their words and actions at a funeral speak of a great appreciation for the sacrifice made, which often cuts lives short. And they are thankful for it as a duty to the country and to those who are able to live without having to sacrifice their lives.

Christian funerals say just as much about our beliefs regarding life, death and salvation. A funeral is the church's opportunity to express those beliefs, to tell the story of the gospel and tie it into the life of the deceased and those gathered to worship.

THE TRADITIONAL CHRISTIAN FUNERAL AND MOURNING RITUALS

The first opportunity most mourners have to be with an extended group of people is at the funeral. Friends and family fly in from around the country. Church members gather together. The visitation and funeral is when mourning, in most respects, begins. Though mourning can begin when a death is foreseen, it only anticipates the actual event. The funeral is when a mourner is for the first time among society as a different person. Between a death and the funeral, families are often caught in the chaos of death. The funeral begins to give shape to grief as the community expresses its faith and ties the swirling emotions following death into the larger story of humanity's fall into sin, redemption and the re-creation of the world. The funeral is an essential element in the mourning process and a chance for the church to, first, begin reintegrating mourners into the community, and second, to publicly express the church's and the deceased's faith and hope.

Early Christian funerals were different from contemporary Jewish or pagan ones, says historian Frederick Paxton. Mourners had a unique sense of the meaning of death as well as the continuation of the life of the Christian community, which incorporated both living and dead. The New Testament books unanimously declare, Paxton writes, that "Jesus rose from the dead not at the end of time but in time, and by his resurrection death had been overcome and the access to paradise lost through Adam's sin regained."[1]

After centuries of Christian tradition, in the last 150 years funerals have slowly lost their Christian emphasis.[2] They became memorial ceremonies calculated simply to soothe the grief of the bereaved rather than being worship services in which a community journeyed to the final resting place of the deceased. Funerals also became the concern of public health officials as cemeteries were moved out of town and new laws regarding the disposal of bodies were passed. As embalming became standard, families needed an expert to take care of the body rather than washing and dressing the body at home. Undertakers began consolidating and coordinating the many services required for a funeral, coffin maker, gravedigger, gathering space, the placement of obituaries.[3] By the twentieth century all these things were being done by the person we now call the funeral director, with the church sometimes playing a specific, secondary role. Christians, along with the rest of society, had ceased to see the process of the funeral as a religiously significant event.

Christians have always incorporated local cultures and particular practices into funerals, but "there is nevertheless a unifying force in the practice of Christian funerals," writes Emory

University professor and preacher Thomas Long: "the gospel narrative." If we are to recover the funeral to its place of significance in the life of the church, we must start here. For in baptism, we were buried in Jesus' death, and we arose in his resurrection. As Paul says in Romans 6:3-5:

> Don't you know that all of us who were baptized into Christ Jesus were baptized into his death? We were therefore buried with him through baptism into death. . . . If we have been united with him like this in his death, we will certainly also be united with him in his resurrection.

The Christian funeral is a worship service that dramatically recognizes "that the Christian life is shaped in the pattern of Christ's own life and death."[4]

A Christian funeral traditionally contained certain elements, rituals that honored the deceased and comforted the sorrowing. During the visitation at home, the family washed, dressed and sat with the body in recognition that it is still created in the image of God and therefore sacred. The visitation was traditionally a period of waiting with the body until it was placed in its final resting place, the last step in its journey before the resurrection. The community visited the home for a period and then began a journey with the body to the grave. The procession stopped for a service at the church, then continued on to accompany the deceased until she was laid to rest. The funeral bound the grieving community together, and it publicly expressed the church's belief in the gospel, that through the resurrected Jesus we have eternal life with God.

The grave was nearby, likely in the churchyard with other relatives, friends and friends' relatives. Mourners could continue to visit and remember the dead, who, the church believed, remained a part of the church community. They were asleep in Christ, awaiting his return and the resurrection. The community had been wounded by death, but it gathered its strength and recovered. Death was not an event to be grieved by a solitary spouse or a handful of children alone.

In this set of funeral rituals—the visitation, procession, funeral and burial—the grieving congregation enacted the stories of the Bible, texts at the heart of the community of faith. Like Mary and the apostle John, who stood at the foot of the cross, Christians attended the dying. Like the woman with the flask of ointment who anointed Jesus and washed his feet with her hair, they prepared the body for burial. They imitated the grieving Christ who mourned at Lazarus's grave and the children of Jacob who interred their father's bones with his ancestors. These physical actions embodied their grief and pointed them, in hope, to the day their beloved dead would rise again.

COMMERCIALIZATION

Today, discussions of funerals—even Christian ones—tend to gravitate toward complaints about price-gouging and exploitative funeral home owners. Funerals are too commercialized and too expensive, many Christians complain. Such grumbles aren't new. Churches once regulated the price gravediggers could charge after mourners complained they were being exploited.

The modern genre of funeral complaints began with a book published in the 1960s that critiqued abuses in the funeral industry and led to needed reforms. Jessica Mitford's *The American Way of Death* pilloried the funeral industry for the ways it took advantage of grieving families, overcharged them and made themselves indispensable while providing few useful functions. Outcry following the book's publication helped pass new laws that forbade abuses such as forcing patrons to purchase a casket only from the funeral home, which might have stocked only expensive and highly profitable ones.

Unfortunately, however, by treating the funeral industry strictly as a consumerist enterprise—in which costs and services are the only factors that matter—Mitford neglected the valuable function that funerals perform for the grieving. And she despised the religious role the funeral played for the faithful. Her book and similar complaints often lay the blame for the problems with modern funerals at the wrong feet.

By critiquing the lack of options provided for consumers and encouraging a get-the-job-done attitude, Mitford helped turn the grieving into consumers and the funeral parlor into a commercial enterprise rather than a site of service to families and individuals in need of community care. Funeral parlors, at least in the popular view, became akin to stores selling grieving paraphernalia.

People now take advantage of all sorts of options to extend their purchasing into the next life. They often feel the whole idea of a funeral is a little morbid, and perhaps a waste of time. Fantasy funerals offer an alternative themed events for golfers, packages for fans of any professional sports team, or films featuring the deceased and made at life's "peak," a time the dead would prefer to be remembered.[5] An article in the *New York Times* explained the trend:

> As members of the baby boom generation plan final services for their parents or themselves, they bring new consumer expectations and fewer attachments to churches, traditions or organ music—forcing funeral directors to be more like party planners, and inviting some party planners to test the farewell waters.[6]

Another trend, pre-death funerals, allows the dead-to-be to enjoy all the considerate words that friends typically offer at a funeral. The pre-deceased can say goodbye and make sure that the funeral goes according to plan.[7] After all, if something goes wrong, there's still time to try again. And why miss the last party to be thrown in your name? Those who object to such materialism or waste of money decide not to have a funeral at all. Or they have an abbreviated ceremony, hiring a cremation service to dispose of the body while friends and family get together at a restaurant or a room in a funeral home. While pragmatic, these options do not allow for the full expression of grief and Christian hope that can be instructive and comforting to those left behind.

A MODEL FUNERAL HOME

While these trends are lamentable, funerals are best done within the context of a church community. Thankfully, many funeral directors do offer needed ministry. For a year I worked at Hultgren Funeral Home in Wheaton, Illinois. I assisted during visitations and funeral services, and I saw how funeral directors are able to work closely with families and help them express their grief in meaningful ways.

Hultgren's funeral directors were all seminary graduates who, after working as pastors, found they were called to practice their ministry at the funeral home. They were glad to pray with families and suggest passages that could be read; they loved to work alongside churches.

Because they believed strongly in working with churches, Hultgren offered a special service to arrange funerals to be done at a church. And since they didn't need to use their own facility, they provided a lower rate and were glad to play second fiddle to the pastor. While he directed the funeral service, Hultgren was happy to provide arrangements, make phone calls and print bulletins.

For those families who took advantage of this personal care, the funeral became a unique event in the spiritual chronology of their lives. Upon arriving to work at a service, I saw how deeply the Hultgren directors cared for families. By handling details and answering questions, Hultgren enabled families to focus on the hard work of grieving that lay before them. It wasn't unusual to see families deeply comforted by the funeral directors. Loved ones called in with questions, stopped by to drop off pictures, personal items or other details for the service. Families often discussed how wonderful the funeral home was—it was a business run with the heart of a ministry. In fact, I often heard families express a deep and heartfelt appreciation for the work of the embalmer who made the deceased look like him- or herself again.

Still, Hultgren could only work within the context provided by families and churches. When there was discord, when there was minimal attachment to a church, when there was little personal context to provide a sense of purpose to the funeral, the work of the funeral home was limited.

A PUBLIC EXPRESSION

When Harry died, people came out of the woodwork. A reserved man, his circle of influence during life had seemed relatively small. But at his visitation the funeral home seemed to be bursting at the seams. Old neighbors, friends of his children and family from out of state returned to pay their respects and support his widowed wife and three grown children. As Harry lay in a casket at one end of the room, surrounded by flowers, those who had loved him in life grieved together and began reknitting their lives without this important thread. Throughout the evening of the visitation, Harry's elderly wife was surrounded by loved ones. Her eyes brightened as more loved ones arrived, and she beamed through tears as she introduced church friends to her great-grandchildren. The atmosphere was heavy with grief. Many shed tears, hugging each other for support. It was clear: Harry had been deeply loved.

Friends and family who gathered for the funeral at the church the next day experienced a full morning of worship with services filled with beloved hymns, Scripture readings, testimonies and a sermon that pointed the grieving to resurrection hope. The faith that had so clearly guided Harry in life was now guiding his loved ones as they sorrowed together in his absence.

A Christian funeral is more than a memorial. The service, of course, does indeed remember the person who has died. This is an important piece of a funeral. It honors the loved one and allows the bereaved to publicly express that person's significance in their lives and in the life of the community. We make a big deal of something that is a big deal. Remembering someone like Harry through a funeral service is a way of saying, "He was important. His life was meaningful, and he will be dearly missed." Saying so also implies that all of our lives have meaning and significance, a fact easily forgotten amid the grief following a loss.

But a Christian funeral does more than that. One funeral director I worked with said he served families best, allowing them to mourn and grieve in the most healthy way, when he was able to bring together all the traditional elements of a visitation and funeral. This allows grieving people to accomplish two things: (1) worship God, who—contrary to our immediate experience of mourning a dead loved one—has defeated death, and (2) re-knit a community that has been fractured.

In some ways a funeral is simply an excuse to publicly get together. Gathering around food, at a funeral home or cemetery, or at-home visitations is an end in itself. A healthy community and the recovering bereaved simply need to be together. Funerals can be done both well and inexpensively, but the purpose is not to get it done cheaply. Singing hymns, reading Scripture and hearing God's Word preached—all with an ear toward the purpose of a funeral—is how the church displays its hope. By doing so the congregation not only gives witness to the rest of the world, but it also serves to reaffirm our resurrection hope.

9

GRIEF AND MOURNING

WHEN C. S. LEWIS WROTE HIS CLASSIC REFLECTIONS on the death of his wife, Joy Davidson, he expressed the isolation, even amidst society, that those who are grieving feel. "An odd by product of my loss," he wrote, "is that I'm aware of being an embarrassment to everyone I meet." At work or in the pub, he said, friends and acquaintances who approached him were unable to say anything without making Lewis painfully aware of their discomfort in talking to him. Though civility required a "hello," these friends gave the impression that they could barely stop themselves from turning their backs the minute they saw him.[1]

Mourning is a complicated process. But it is necessary, and it must be properly done for a person to successfully recover from the death of a loved one. Grieving is active work. The grieving person needs to come to terms with his or her loss, recognizing the fact of the loved one's death. This, by itself, is a difficult task and one that even viewing a corpse may not completely help achieve. Once the fact of the loss is recognized, the mourner must mourn—weep, wail and agonize. And finally, out of the depths of the traumatic severing of a beloved relationship, the

mourner must slowly rebuild a life as a new person. Mourners
will suffer the death of all the ways they have absorbed the char-
acters of their loved ones. All the ways one person relies on another must be taken up for oneself. This takes time and a great
deal of healing.

TRADITIONS OF MOURNING

Lewis's England was a particularly inhospitable place for the bereaved. An academic at the time studied the British attitude toward death, and in his book titled *The Pornography of Death,* Geof-
frey Gorer said modern Britons ignored death in the same way
their Victorian ancestors avoided sex. Indeed, British children
did not attend funerals, and families often treated death as they
did Christmas, an imaginary and fairytale event. Writing two
decades later, French historian Phillipe Aries described the way
parents taught their children "that their father has gone on a trip
or that Jesus has taken him. Jesus," he wrote, "has become a kind
of Santa Claus whom adults use to tell children about death without believing in him themselves."[2]

This denial of death was a strange reversal following the Victorians' sentimentalization of it. In the 1800s it was common to pose
for photographs with the beloved's corpse. The bereaved sometimes visited the corpse, if it wasn't buried, for weeks or months
and observed the decay, and they mourned in other ways that
might astonish us today. But the effects of war, medical technology
and other social opinions created dramatic changes in the second
half of the nineteenth century and first half of the twentieth.

When society ignored death, children grew up with no sense
of the meaning of death and became adults with no understanding of the proper behavior toward the grieving. Lewis felt this
keenly in the days after his loss. "Perhaps the bereaved ought to

be isolated in special settlements like lepers," he wrote. "To some, I'm worse than an embarrassment. I am a death's head [a skull]. Whenever I meet a happily married pair I can feel them both thinking 'One or other of us must some day be as he is now.'"[3] As if the burdens of the griever weren't enough, society gave Lewis another responsibility—the cruel job of forcing a man in mourning to help those around him feel better about their awkwardness in his presence.

In the United States things were little different. By the 1950s the country had given up the mourning rituals that were common fifty years before, such as distinctive dress for women, black armbands for men or decorations outside the home signaling that the family inside was in mourning. Mourning was a job for the group. Those in mourning openly signaled their grief by wearing clothing or jewelry that let everyone know of their status as bereaved. This put the burden on others, not the mourner, to ease social interactions, to comfort and to allow the open expression of grief.

"All the changes that have modified attitudes toward death in the past thousand years," Aries writes, "have not altered this fundamental image, this permanent relationship between death and society." Yet, in one short century, it ended. As C. S. Lewis discovered, the grieving are desperately alone.

In 1984 a journalist reporting on widows of Vietnam found that "The overwhelming majority [of people surveyed] thought that individuals should be through mourning between 48 hours and two weeks after a death."[4] Though Americans no longer deny death as they once did, and efforts like the hospice movement have done much to help people die and grieve well, Christians are a long way from being of any more use to the grieving than C. S. Lewis's friends.

THE PROCESS OF GRIEF

Lewis's experience is not too different from that of many people today who have lost a loved one. Today, grieving is often a lonely, awkward experience. Nevertheless, grieving well is best done within a supportive community that is willing to suffer, wait and care for the person devastated by a loss, and who in many ways is a new person. It is a tragedy that, for many, such a community doesn't exist. In our fractured society it is not our natural inclination to be this sort of community, and we may be past middle age before we need to become this sort of community.

Grieving well begins with dying well. Survivors have plenty to overcome as they mourn the loss of a loved one. A good death helps begin that process. This process is clinically and popularly described as occurring in stages. First comes disbelief, then yearning for the dead loved one, anger, depression and finally acceptance. In February 2007 the *Journal of the American Medical Association* published a report by the Yale Bereavement Study, which largely confirmed the popular notion of these stages during recovery from grief: including denial, anger, bargaining and finally acceptance. (It is important to note that the "stages" of grief may be better described as moods that come and go throughout the mourning process even if they occur more frequently at certain points.)

The Yale study found that feelings of yearning peaked four months after a loss, to be followed by anger. At six months came increased feelings of depression. Typically, the occurrence of the first four stages significantly declined after six months as the bereaved gained acceptance of the loss. Though the first six months are the most traumatic, the grieving process typically takes two years,[5] though it may take twice as long before a survivor feels as though life has reached a "new normal."

THE DANGER OF INTERRUPTION

Mourning is a natural process: first the shock, then the deep grief and finally the slow rebuilding of a new life. But the process can be interrupted. "The danger with grief at bereavement is that, having surrendered to it, as willy-nilly at first we must, we should never get beyond it," writes J. I. Packer. More communal societies have ritualized ways of leading the mourner safely through this process, but in the West, writes Packer, it has become more and more difficult "for mourners to regain a life that is more than performance while deep down the heart still aches."[6]

Susan Zonnebelt-Smeenge and Robert DeVries became experts on grieving after both of their spouses died in 1993 and 1994. Since marrying each other, they have sought to help other Christians deal with grief in a healthy and biblical way. When her husband died, Susan said, "It just was harder than I ever imagined." As a clinical psychologist Susan had worked with a number of patients who had lost a spouse. Still, she found the process incredibly more difficult than expected.

While her Christian faith helped Susan through the process, she discovered that knowing a few things at the outset would have helped her grieve. The bereaved, she says, will need to work through the grieving process. While life cannot be postponed, working through grief is the most important job for at least the first year following a loss.

Christians have the advantage of believing in a God who can support the mourner, Susan says. On the often solitary journey of grief, it can be helpful "to know that God understands, and God can take your anger at him or your confusion or whatever kind of feelings you have. You're not walking this alone."

However, it will feel very solitary. "It is a pretty solo and

lonely journey a lot of the time," Susan says. "Even though it
helps to have people come alongside of you and say they care, it
really is each individual griever's journey. Traveling through
grief, everybody has their own individual stamp on how that's
going to look, because every person is a very unique person."

Robert DeVries, a professor emeritus at Calvin Theological
Seminary, says that Christians have assistance as they work
through grief. We have the hope of heaven. The Bible promises
that we will be with God and with those who love him after we
die. This fact can give Christians an abiding sense of joy and
peace even in the midst of mourning.

However, Robert says, that hope can sometimes be used inap-
propriately. We do rejoice in Jesus' victory over death, which
gives us the hope of heaven and the comfort of knowing that
those we love are resting with God. However, those in mourning and their comforters may make grieving more difficult when
our Christian hope is used to discourage public mourning.
Mourners can use heaven as an excuse to avoid necessary pain,
pretending that the loss of death isn't real because we will be
reunited with our loved ones in heaven. Christians sometimes
impose a kind of ban on mourning, using the hope of heaven as
an excuse to avoid being confronted with someone else's pain.

As Christians, Robert says, "We talk a lot about eternal life
and about being in heaven, and at funerals we often use that as
some form of comfort. But the flip side of that is to be very careful as a griever not to use heaven as a way to deflect from the
actual grief that you experience."

Death is real; there is no need to say that because our loved
one is in heaven, death doesn't exist. Death is a fact, and its sting
is painful. So we mourn. But death has been defeated, and, comforted by the Holy Spirit, we ask with the apostle Paul, "Death,

where is thy sting? O grave, where is thy victory?" (1 Corinthians 15:55 KJV).

While we do not mourn as those who have no hope, we do mourn. "We advocate understanding biblical lament," Robert says. "Though heaven is a real place, we do lament here on earth."

"A lot of folks think that Christianity simply has to be joy, victory, peace and comfort." When Christians don't allow for true lament, they can cut short the grieving process. "You will have trouble in this world, Jesus says. You've got to understand and accept that," says Robert. "Blessed are those who mourn."

Proper grieving takes time, and taking that time recognizes the importance of the person's life. When two people, husband and wife, parent and child, brother and sister, close friends, have intertwined their lives together, it takes time to undo those ties. The grief process acknowledges the depth of the relationship. "A lot of people assume that you are going to want to go back to what you had before," Robert says. "You don't go back to what it had been before." Mourning is the transition from one life with a person we loved to another life without that person.

Any person who loses a loved one needs to recognize, Susan says, "I was attached to this person. I walked through life with this person, and this person has interwoven his or her life with mine. I'm hurting in all the ways that this person was in my life. I have to make some really major adjustments." Doing this takes time, and those in mourning should not allow others to hurry them through this process.

"Our society," says Susan, "wants to make it easy on everybody." We rush along the grieving process, encouraging people to move on or sending subtle expectations that a person in mourning should return to life as before. Like C. S. Lewis's friends, death makes us feel so awkward that we push the grieving person to "act normal" again. This behavior doesn't recognize "that when we do that we're actually making it harder for that person to work through grief, because facing pain heals it."

"We think that, from a Christian perspective, if a grieving person gets back and sings in the choir or teaches Sunday school again that will be a good sign," Susan says. Unfortunately, getting back to the old things may be simply a distraction from doing the work of grieving. Churches too often play a role in distracting mourners from grieving, rather than helping them along that journey, Susan says. "Churches are much more available when people are dying than when people are grieving, and a lot of people feel that the church just doesn't acknowledge them any longer [when they don't quickly return to their old ways]."

CAN WE DO THAT?

Lauren Winner, an author and professor at Duke Divinity School, discovered modern churches' stark absence of mourning rituals after converting from Judaism to Christianity. In her book *Mudhouse Sabbath,* Winner writes of missing the mourning rituals of her Jewish faith. "The chapter on grief," says Winner, "is the chapter by far that people respond to the most. It's the chapter I still get mail from people saying, 'How can Christians do this kind of communal bereavement process?'"

In the nineteenth century, says Winner, Christians also practiced mourning in a similarly intentional way. Among other things, the Victorians and Americans of the era wore mourning clothes and jewelry. These Victorian traditions expressed the view that what a person wore signaled something beyond a person's fashion sense. "When I dress in mourning," Winner says, "I'm both telling myself that I'm bereaved, and I'm also making it communal." Mourning clothes provide a signal that placed the burden on those who were not grieving. "It really is the opposite of the modern stance in which a bereaved person is praised for getting back to work in a week," she says. In response the community is signaled to reach out in comfort and concern.

Mourners need to be able to communicate to the community that they are in need of special consideration. And the community needs to be willing to receive those signals. Rather than reinstituting mourning dress codes, churches could provide these signals in other ways. In the church bulletin, rather than simply listing mourners in need of prayer during the week of or following a death, churches could keep their names printed for a full year. The church could mark the anniversary of a death during a service or by offering coffee and donuts on a Sunday in honor of the deceased. A church team might be designated to provide one meal a month during the year following a death. The meal wouldn't be provided because one can't cook while grieving, but simply because the church needs an excuse to get together and show their concern.

Mourning rituals need not be elaborate or expensive. The goal is not necessarily to produce a display in someone's honor but to simply provide everyone in the community the opportunity to recognize a loss. Cards, meals and public announcements are ways of saying that an important member of our community is suffering and in need of our care.

JEWISH MOURNING RITUALS

The Old Testament has plenty of instructions on caring for widows, and by extension, anyone in mourning. Deuteronomy 14:28-29 says that widows are entitled to the nation's tithes so that they "may come and eat and be satisfied, and so that the LORD your God may bless you." Psalm 68 says God is a "defender of widows," and in Jeremiah 49 the Lord says, "Your widows too can trust in me."

Due in part to these commands, the Jewish tradition has developed an elaborate set of rituals to guide the mourning process. Although Jews are not necessarily any better at always following their traditions than Christians are, the set of rituals following a death are becoming popular even among nonpracticing Jews. There are many ways that churches can learn from them.

Following the funeral, mourners begin one week of shiva. During these seven days, the mourner is to do nothing but grieve. The congregation visits throughout the week and every day says prayers. The mourner is not to clean the house or him- or herself. Neither is the mourner to cook, change clothes or play host to guests. The congregation brings the mourner's food. "If death is not something to be marked for a week because it is so awesome an event," says Rabbi Jack Reimer, "if death is nothing, if death is cheap, then life is cheap."[7] Because life is not cheap, the Jewish tradition takes very seriously the time of mourning, especially the shiva. This period allows the mourner to let go and succumb to death's devastation. But the continuous presence of the community sustains the mourner's ties to others. And its prayers sustain communion with God.

After a week it is time to rejoin the community. This reunion is in some ways forced on the mourner, because otherwise it may not happen. The mourner joins others who mourn by saying Kaddish, communal prayer, twice a day for the next eleven months. The immersion back into the community—a community of other mourners specifically—can be extremely helpful. Meeting twice daily is a sort of spiritual support group with mourners' needs as the focus. Those who are working through their own grief are best able to help those newly grieving. The twice-daily prayer also helps those whose anger, because of their loss, may turn into anger at God. Affirming one's faith twice daily is a powerful antidote to doubt at a time when it is most likely to creep in. On the one-year anniversary of the death, Yahrzeit, the mourner says Kaddish again.

After a year the formal work of mourning is over. But the community still commemorates those who have died. Four times a year special services are held, during which all those who have not lost an immediate family member may be asked to leave. The services remember all those who have died. This is the community of the bereaved, to which the mourner always belongs. This tradition helps the community take care of its widows, widowers and other mourners. It also ensures that the community will always know how to do so. "When we have a problem," says Rabbi Riemer, "we can look up what those who came before us think we should do."[8]

Christians can learn much from Jewish mourning rituals in the way they allow the mourner time and space to feel the full force of loss, yet work to reintegrate the mourner back into the community and back to God. Because of the resurrection these mourning actions, while expressing the devastation of loss, are for Christians infused with hope. In Christianity death is not the end but a transition to a better, fuller life. Though Christians may find more hope in their understanding of the meaning of death and life, the Jewish rituals can be powerful.

BEYOND GRIEF

As surely and certainly as we hope in the resurrection of the dead, that is not the only reason Christians are to mourn differently than those who do not believe in a Savior who will redeem their bodies. As theologian and bishop of Durham N. T. Wright makes clear over and over again, the world to come is not completely separate from this one. Indeed, Jesus lives in a resurrected body even now. And the life of the God who raised Jesus from the dead lives within the Christian. So, while we wait for death's final defeat, the beginning of that defeat in our own life begins in our salvation. In our journey through life—and through dying and death—we can find joy for we have a sure and certain hope in the redemption of our bodies. Second, we have access in this life to the power of the resurrection that gives us comfort from our grief.

As C. S. Lewis recovered from the devastation that followed his wife's death, he began to think differently about how he should have mourned her. His journal, which became the book *A Grief Observed,* had been chiefly about himself, he said, then his wife, and finally about God. "In that order," he wrote. And that order was the inverse of what it should have been. Never, he wrote, did he begin to praise either Joy or God. Yet, Lewis says, "Praise is the mode of love which always has some element of joy in it. . . . Don't we in praise somehow enjoy what we praise, however far we are from it?"[9]

It is no easy task to move from the shock, anger and depression of the beginning of grief to the joy and praise that, with God, we can experience. Of course joy and praise can exist alongside ongoing pain and yearning for the departed beloved. As Walter Wangerin Jr., a Lutheran pastor, writes, "even the weeping at weddings, is grief. When we die, we grieve."[10]

Death, Wangerin says, is the breaking of any relationship. The first death was the Fall. And throughout our lives we die all kinds of small deaths. And we learn to grieve. We grieve at the ending of the relationship with our childhood sweetheart, when we leave home, as our children grow up, when our parents can no longer care for themselves. If we don't resist the grief, we will find healing in the pain. "Grief is the grace of God within us, the natural process of recovery for those who have suffered death," Wangerin writes.[11]

This is the essence of the gospel: Jesus brought God to humans, repairing the death of the Fall; and Jesus, rising from the dead, brought humans to God, ending the grief caused by the pain of our separation from God. If this good news means something more than hope in the by-and-by, if it means something right now, it means that God is with us in our grief and able to redeem it too.

Christianity does not shrink from death. It does not force a smile on the grieving. Christianity does not ignore death or say that it means nothing. Death is the last enemy, says Paul. It is evil, the greatest and most complete of evils. And if Christians are to know the greatness of Jesus Christ's victory over death, they must know that death is evil.

Joy and sorrow, writes Wangerin, are not opposites. "It is through sorrow that one discovers a calm, abiding, indestructible joy." Our faith offers us this paradox, that a seed must fall into the ground and die before it produces fruit. "Death leads to life," says Wangerin, "And grief is the road between them."[12] Mourning, aided by the rituals of a church community, allows those who are swallowed by grief to slowly journey along that road.

NO ROAD MAP

"Grief just is. There aren't necessarily rights and wrongs," says Rob Bugh, pastor of Wheaton Bible Church in Wheaton, Illinois. A trim and energetic man, Bugh is still holding back the depth of his pain.

Despite years as a pastor, Rob discovered grief anew when, three months after a close friend died, Rob's wife, Carol, was diagnosed with cancer. Grief, Rob said nine months after Carol's death, is an "emotional, visceral response to pain, suffering, tragedy and death."

Carol's death came just eleven months after her diagnosis, and that time was filled with doctor's visits, hospital stays, long-distance travel to specialists, and trips to the emergency room.

Rob says he was unprepared for the turn his life was taking. "One of my closest friends and my wife, they're both getting horrific news. Their cancers are different, but they're ravaging their bodies. And they're brutal. How do you wrap your mind around that?"

"I'm in ministry," Rob says. "I take care of people going through this, but I really never thought this would happen to us."

Carol had turned fifty, and on a regular doctor visit she asked about some bleeding in her stool. Doctors performed tests, and the diagnosis was a rare form of rectal cancer. It was aggressive, and the Bughs fought it aggressively. But, as Rob says, they never received good news. Eventually they started running out of options. They continued trying new treatments, visiting doctors, seeking and hoping for a cure.

"Early on," Rob says, "you're 100 percent fighting." But slowly, "There's a growing awareness that God may be up to something else than bringing about healing." They didn't stop treatments, they continued hoping for a cure, yet gradually the realization dawned that there may be none. "There's this resignation that comes," Rob says. "Now you know what the gospel describes at Gethsemane when Jesus says, 'Take this cup from me.' That was a passage I prayed over and over, 'God take this from us. Take this cancer from us, but not my will but thy will be done.'"

The final three months were hectic and incredibly stressful, and the couple had little time to talk about Carol's death. And the end came much quicker than they had expected. Two days before Carol died, the family took her home and brought in hospice. And then, "all of a sudden it was all over."

Though her death was horrible, tumors grew all over her upper body inside and outside her skin, Carol died well. "My wife was amazing during this," Bugh says, "because she never complained, and she was always very positive. Now was she scared? Was she worried? Yeah, but she had a firm conviction in the sovereignty of God. She was a deeply spiritual woman. We didn't like it, but we were willing to accept this as God's assignment for our life. Carol never lasted in self-pity."

Not only did Carol bravely face her trial, but she thought of what she wanted to say to her family, before her death. She had prepared letters to be given after her death to every member of her family. In the chaos of hospital visits and treatments, Carol found time to write down her last words to those she loved. "She wrote me an amazing letter," Rob says. "She was profound. She said three things. She said, 'You have no regrets in our marriage. You've been a great husband. You've been faithful.' The second thing she said was, 'You will make it.' And the third thing was, 'I want you to remarry.'"

Carol's striking foresight recalls the Christian tradition of last words. And Carol's words were so insightful, Bugh said, that she gave him the room necessary to launch the family into a new life without her. This also gave Bugh the opportunity to grieve. He had no regrets, no concerns plaguing him beyond the devastating loss of his wife.

As pastor of one of the largest churches in the area, Bugh also had the responsibility of grieving publicly. The advantage was that his family had an enormous amount of support. "The community rallied," Bugh says. "The downside is there are moments where you just want to run into a cave and hide and just sob. Just sob."

"If I stand up and just talk about God's sovereignty, there are going to be people in the pews that think, Oh man, he feels so good, and I feel so crummy. What's the matter with me?" Instead, Bugh told his congregation, "This is terrible, and I've had moments where I have just felt utter despair. But yet I do believe God is sovereign, and I have this contentment."

Bugh still misses his wife terribly. "We had an extraordinary marriage," he says, "And it's gone. This woman that I did life with is gone. But yet I'm okay. That's God's grace."

The loss was "more brutal than I could have imagined. Yet God's grace is much richer, much deeper, much more profound, much more real than I would have ever thought."

10

A CULTURE
OF RESURRECTION

In 2004, at a regular staff meeting at *Christianity Today,* we learned that Fred Smith, a leading figure behind a number of Christian ministries, including that of *Christianity Today,* was in the hospital and likely to die within days. It was a situation we encountered frequently. The evangelical awakening after World War II had produced a number of men and women who started or significantly increased the scope of parachurch ministries, such as Campus Crusade, World Vision, the Billy Graham Evangelistic Association and a number of others. Fifty years later those evangelical entrepreneurs were elderly and many were dying.

The son of a pastor, Smith became a businessman during the Great Depression. He was president of a division of Genesco, at the time the largest apparel company in the world. But having grown up in a family dedicated to full-time Christian work, Smith was able to apply his unique sense of business efficiency and operations to ministries that were high on passion and motivation but low on thoughtful and strategic use of their resources. His insights were keen and poignant, usually cutting to the heart of an issue, yet full of humor. In addition to running Genesco operations, Smith served on the boards of Youth for Christ, Christianity Today and other organizations.

As Fred Smith got older, he retired from business and became less involved in actively overseeing Christian ministries. Rather than spending his sunset years on the golf course or on Caribbean cruises, Smith entered a new stage of kingdom service. He expanded the one-on-one mentoring that had characterized his professional life. He mentored a number of leaders, providing a sounding board for ideas and spiritual guidance for leaders who needed an unbiased peer. It was a ministry Smith had always performed, but mentoring took on new significance in his final years. Rather than seeking rest and comfort during his golden years, Smith focused even more on the mission he set for himself in his twenties. He even broadened this personal ministry by launching a website and forming an online community of those who were eager to learn from him. It was quite an accomplishment for a ninety-year-old man.

Smith's late-life ministry followed the pattern he had established from an early age. At twenty-eight, Smith thought of what he would want said about him on his tombstone. "He stretched others," Smith decided would be the motto of his life. So, into his nineties, and as his kidneys began to fail, Smith would host regular conference calls on the days he would be required to spend most of his time hooked up to dialysis machines.

As I wrote Smith's obituary, assuming we would need to publish it soon, I became fascinated by Smith's story and his commonsense wisdom. I checked his "Breakfast with Fred" website regularly both to read Smith's posts and Smith's family's updates on his health.

Surprising many, little by little, Smith returned to health. At more than ninety years old and after a lifetime of service to people and the church, Smith wasn't finished. Eventually, he resumed his mentoring phone calls and webposts, and Smith lived for another three years. During that time, with the help of his daughter, he also wrote a book, *Breakfast with Fred,* published just as he died.

Smith's last book, though clearly written by someone whose health forced him to look death in the eye, is not about dying well or aging well. Instead it is about living well. The values he carried with him throughout life gave Fred Smith the foundation for a good death. A key element of dying well is to maintain the relationships and meaningful activities that are a significant part of life.

The Christian's ability to face the temptations and problems that arrive alongside death come from living a good life. The difficulties of aging, frailty and the end of life are not the result of challenges unique to the final years. Rather, living well requires values and an approach to life that are also essential to dying well. Those values Smith espoused as a leader of corporations and director of several ministries were the same he wrote about in the final two years of his life.

These values of living well need to be carried through to the end of life. The virtue of loving our neighbor and the priority of family relationships and friendships over career ambitions can be both taught and strengthened at the end of life—even by someone with a terminal illness. For those of us who require the disciplining of life's hard knocks to instill biblical values and a Christian sense of rightful living, the process of gradual dying offers the opportunity to learn how to live and die well. For others, it is the opportunity to live those values more deeply. This happens best when we are connected to the church.

AGING IN THE TWENTY-FIRST CENTURY

As it has done in so many other aspects of our lives, modern medicine has radically changed what it means to grow old. Previous centuries had their share of elderly. There's nothing new about growing old itself. But never before has an entire population expected to become old and to live for decades as an "old person." Well into the twentieth century, most people retired only after they could physically no longer work. And retirement rarely lasted long. Today, we think of retirement as a time to reap the benefits of forty years of work. We expect to travel, pursue a hobby, take up golf, visit grandkids. Westerners spend their working lives squirreling away money so they can live and enjoy twenty-five or more years of work-free life. No other generation in human history has had such an expectation.

This kind of extended life also means that we can all expect to observe our bodies' slow decline. Gradual dying will be an earmark of these upcoming generations. "We are in the midst of a demographic shift unprecedented in history," said Dr. Richard J. Hodes, former director of the National Institutes of Health in his 2005 budget request. At a time when the United States was about to claim 300 million citizens, there were 35 million people older than sixty-five. There are more elderly people today, he wrote, "than at any other time in history." Among those over age sixty-five, there were four million older than eighty-five and sixty-five thousand who had celebrated their one-hundredth birthday.

Over the next quarter-century, Hodes predicted, the number of elderly Americans would double to more than seventy million and make up 20 percent of the population, up from 13 percent in 2005. The fastest-growing age group is that above eighty-five, who are the most at risk for illness and disability. "Their ranks are expected to grow from 4.3 million in 2000 to at least 19.4 million in 2050," estimated Hodes.[1]

This, the fastest growing demographic, is also the sickest, putting intense pressure on families, health care providers and insurers. Adults now turning sixty-five will need an average of three years of long-term care—feeding, clothing, bathing, medicine—before death. Most will rely on family members for that care. A recent study by the National Alliance for Caregiving and the AARP found that 44 million people (21 percent of the U.S. population) are family caregivers. Two-thirds of these caregivers are women.[2] Many elderly patients, 35 percent, will receive care from a nursing home. A few will require as much as five years of full-time professional nursing care, probably in a facility outside the home.[3] Of those already sixty-five or older, 10 percent has that devastating disease, Alzheimer's. Half of those over eighty-five have the disease.[4]

CHANGING A MINDSET

Rather than see these statistics as a burden, churches need to regard these individuals as a vital part of their congregations, including them in church life until their last breath. Not only is the church called to do precisely this—care for widows and all the elderly in need—but because the whole congregation is edified and formed when we care for the old and the dying, we learn to die well by seeing others do it first.

Receiving and giving spiritual care in the midst of a congregation is essential to dying well. Studies show that an active spiritual life provides people the strength to positively and productively face these challenging final years. In other words, those elderly able to continue living well, with fulfilling personal relationships and a rich spiritual life, are well prepared to die well.

Our churches have not been particularly successful at creating places where the dying can live out a full life in their final years. In a magazine for pastors, an advertisement for a book about a new theological trend declared readers would learn "how to grow a younger body." The playful jab at anti-aging cosmetics, which so often promise to do the same, reveals a less humorous reality in many of our churches. As congregations age and pastors focus on attracting younger members, the elderly—and certainly the dying—are dismissed as less desirable.

In a society in which intergenerational ties are already weak, it takes some education and practice to help people overcome the differences one finds between the generations. If the gap between middle-age adults and the elderly is difficult to bridge, then the chasm between pastors and the dying can be even greater.

WHO'S TO BLAME?

If we tend to work with what we know, a brief glance at a seminary course schedule eliminates any wonder about why churches seem less attracted to caring for the dying. Classes on youth and family ministry abound. However, even where we would expect spiritual care for the dying to be taught, it is absent. Seminaries—where those who minister to the dying receive training to do so—often entirely neglect teaching spiritual care for the elderly and dying.

Ian Knox, a lawyer turned evangelist, studied church attitudes toward the elderly in Britain and noted a significant lack of clergy training for the elderly and dying. In one denomination, "there are special sessions on work with children and young people— but nothing relating to older people," writes Knox. When Knox asked if there was training for future pastors for work with people over sixty-five, he was told there was none. The denominational seminary made one concession to the spiritual needs of the elderly and dying: a two-hour lecture about older people.[5]

Following the health crisis of the president of a major evangelical seminary, I asked a friend, who was scheduled to interview him, to see if his views on training pastors had changed. It had changed dramatically, and only with my friend's question did the seminary president begin to think about the lack of training those future pastors received when it came to caring for the dying. The president had never until then thought about including such training at the seminary—though after his health crises he was suddenly interested in doing so.

At another seminary, spiritual care for the dying was included only within a discussion of ethical issues related to end-of-life medical care—so that pastors could help families decide when to remove life support and navigate other treacherous waters. Even there, one professor who taught a class exclusively on end-of-life issues lamented that while students studying many different subjects, such as psychology or education, enrolled, "I've never had a pastoral student [in the class]. But I would love to."

If our churches are not helping us to think about these things, it is, in part, because our seminarians do not train for these things. They cut their teeth in the youth group, not the nursing home. We don't require pastors to help us die. This negligence has pushed the dying away from the church. "People who are sick don't think about calling the pastor," says John Dunlop, "because they have never been schooled that's an area the pastor needs to be involved in. And the pastor's not comfortable being involved."

Some pastors believe it is not the job of the church to accommodate the needs of the elderly, but it is the responsibility of the elderly to fit into the church. "We want older people to grow and move" in order for the church to be attractive to young people, one bishop told Knox. He wanted the elderly "to stay young and fresh,"[6] Perhaps that is why, in Knox's interviews with dozens of church and seminary leaders as well as church members, no one "spoke of helping older people to face their own death."[7]

Nevertheless, caring for the elderly, the ill and the dying has always been a basic function of the church. Today, families are in particular need for the church to assist in that responsibility. Caregivers need the church's help to do the things that need doing: trips to the doctor, cooking, cleaning, navigating the medical maze or simply getting a break from all these things. Beyond material assistance, the dying need to know they still matter to the church body. Particularly in a culture where dying may take two or more years to complete, this relationship needs to be intentional.

Lest we lay the burden solely at the feet of church leaders, Knox found a striking ignorance not only of how to minister to older adults but an ignorance even of how many elderly attended their churches. "Virtually no one in any church or denomination seemed to have any idea of how many older people belonged to either," he writes.[8] We cannot depend on pastors to take up the responsibility alone. As we look for ways to serve the church, we too must be intentional about seeking out the dying and their families, learning how to love them in this unique hour and actively caring for them in tangible ways.

A POSITIVE VISION

The Bible is full of examples of the elderly living out their faith in the fullness of their years. In the New Testament, Simeon worked in the temple, awaiting the fulfillment of God's promise that he would not die before seeing the Messiah. His faithfulness to the work of God was rewarded when he held the infant Jesus in his arms. In that moment he sensed that his remaining time on earth was short. As he gazed at the infant Messiah, he prayed, "Sovereign Lord, now let your servant die in peace, as you have promised" (Luke 2:29 NLT).

Like Simeon, as our church members grow old and die gradually, they still have potential for significant service in the church. They are our matriarchs and patriarchs, vessels filled with life's wisdom and examples to younger generations. Even as they are dying, like Fred Smith, they can lead, instruct, exhort, pray and witness. As we continue to weave the aging and those who are slowly dying into the life of the congregation, their participation in the body of Christ will enhance our (and their) living and guide our dying.

Before the church can directly minister with and to the dying, it must first shift its perception of older members' contributions to the church in their later years. For many churches the first step in helping the elderly and dying live meaningfully at the end of their lives is to rethink our vision of retirement. People work hard, live frugally and, when they retire, are ready to enjoy their sunset years—the last chapter in life filled with regular rounds of golf, frequent vacations and perhaps move to a warmer climate. "In our culture this often means disengaging not only from the workplace but from the church and the community," says gerontologist John Dunlop. This disengagement becomes particularly difficult when an elderly person is diagnosed with a terminal illness. Without roots in a community, without the regular connections at church, an elderly person who served the church faithfully in younger years may find himself without support as he is dying.

As a unique, intergenerational community, the church can offer a new kind of retirement to elderly members, a kind of retirement plan that will go with them, as they will move through their last years from health to frailty to dying. By encouraging the elderly and the dying to use their gifts for ministry in the church, the church imparts value to these later years and helps the aging to maintain a vital connection to the community—a connection they will rely on heavily when they are dying.

FOLLOWING IN THE STEPS OF THE EARLY CHURCH

Early Christians made elderly widows a specific order in the church. "The *Apostolic Constitutions* specifies that deaconesses are to be chosen from the widows and to be ordained with the laying on of hands."[9] They were both cared for by the church, as Scripture consistently commands, and they administered specific functions of the church. The apostle Paul gave direct commands in 1 Timothy as to who was qualified for this position. Those women who had lost a loved one were looked to as examples in the church. Women who had journeyed through grief were well qualified to teach the younger saints, among other things, about "bringing up children, showing hospitality, washing the feet of the saints, helping those in trouble" (1 Timothy 5:10).

These elderly Christians had spiritual responsibilities to their congregation. Paul says in Titus that older women should "teach what is good. Then they can train the younger women to love their husbands and children, to be self-controlled and pure, to be busy at home, to be kind, and to be subject to their husbands, so that no one will malign the word of God" (Titus 2:3-5).

Retirement can provide those with the time an opportunity for spiritual pursuits that may not have been possible in busier days. Even in the face of a terminal illness, an elderly Christian like Fred Smith can admonish the saints, pray and engage in other spiritual disciplines that add value to the congregation. Dying in many cases is no longer an event in someone's life but rather a period of time. Concentration on prayer, Bible reading, service and other spiritual disciplines prepares a person's heart for transitioning to life in eternity, and it can be a source of spiritual strength for a congregation and for a family.

Paul's vision here and elsewhere in his epistles is one of a community in which the younger generations benefit from the experience and wisdom of their elders. Such a community has two elements that many of ours lack. First, the elderly are integrated into the congregation. When members are actively dying and professional health care takes them away from the congregation to a nursing home or assisted living facility, it is the church that must go to them. "The best care we can give the aged is, when possible, to use their gifts," writes Rowan Greer, "This means trying to avoid segregating the aged or at least seeking to mitigate that isolation as much as we can. We can strive to enable the aged to keep on serving, to be needed."[10]

Whether present or absent from the assembled body, the dying remain a vital part of the congregation, not relegated solely to the care of a nursing home chaplain. This may require reworking our ministries to accommodate elderly dying members. Small group members who once may have bid farewell to a member who enters a nursing home can decide to move their weekly meetings to the dying member's bedside. A key leader diagnosed with a terminal illness may, instead of simply stepping down from the finance committee, be enlisted as a prayer warrior for the committee—dedicating his hours at treatments to praying for the ministry of the church. The church can encourage this kind of transition by providing a list of prayer requests along with the encouragement that the finance committee member is also being prayer for.

Second, Paul's vision assumes intergenerational respect. Our rapidly changing society has resulted in succeeding generations who grow up in radically different circumstances. One generation's experience may produce a fundamentally different outlook on life than a previous generation, generating conflict. Older people may be viewed as out of touch with reality or hopelessly stuck in the past. Yet Paul sees that older women and men can teach younger people what it means to live a good Christian life. If we are to relearn what it means to die, our churches must intentionally include the elderly and dying. We and our children will learn to live and die well from the faithful witness of dying believers in our midst.

This intergenerational community provides not only healthy instruction to the young but also purpose to the old. For the elderly, and for anyone facing death, "community is huge," says Al Weir, vice president for campus and community ministries at the Christian Medical and Dental Association. "There's no emotional healing that takes place outside of community." People who are chronically ill, debilitated or simply elderly and frail tend to lose whatever community they may have had. This is uniquely true for the elderly, who over the years tend to lose their community and church connections. They no longer visit the VFW hall, play bridge together or even attend church. When they are dying, they often are even more secluded. It is essential that families and churches find ways for these dear saints to remain integrated in their communities.

Everyone needs to have a sense of mission and meaning. Fred Smith exemplified this when he remained connected to his mentoring community and even expanded his reach as a mentor as he became more ill and nearer to death. "A tremendous source of value just leaks out of people's lives," Weir says, when they're allowed to think that all they have left in life is their death. "I think God's not through with us till he takes us home," he says, and Christians need to put a sense of mission back into the lives of the elderly and the very ill. "If we can," Weir says, "they have this vitality that returns and remains to the end of their days."

ELDERLY ACCOMPLISHMENTS

Having this sense of mission, Weir says, empowers even the dying to be able to do great things for God. A nurse Weir once worked with, Melanie, told him the story of her father. Larry Sanders loved to go on mission trips, and he particularly loved the country of Guyana on the northern South American coast. But Sanders, when he was older, developed cancer. The cancer forced doctors to remove one of his legs, and because the cancer spread to his lungs, he had to carry an oxygen tank with him in order to boost the supply to his lungs. Still, on crutches and with a tank strapped to him, Sanders told his family, "I think God wants me to go back to Guyana."

His family, naturally, was opposed to the trip. It's a rough country, and he would be far from adequate medical care in case of an emergency. They tried to persuade him against the idea. "I don't care," he replied. "I think God wants me to go, and I'm going to go."

As expected, the trip was difficult and exhausting. So much so, in fact, that soon after his return, Larry Sanders died. He had completed his last mission trip and followed his heart even with one leg and bad lungs. The trip amazed his family, friends and church, and it gave Larry's final days purpose and meaning. Yet Sanders's presence in Guyana paid far more eternal dividends.

Years later, Melanie, Larry's daughter, heard an unusual story. A friend who had moved away returned for a visit, and she told Melanie about a Bible study in her new Arkansas town. At one of their gatherings the members relayed how they became Christians. Eventually, it was a woman's turn who spoke with a strange accent. The young lady began, "I'm from the country of Guyana." She continued, "My parents came to know Christ many years ago from missionaries that came there, but I never thought it was very important until one day a crippled man came. He had only one leg, and he was wearing an oxygen tank. He could hardly get up the hill. When I saw him come to tell me about the gospel, I knew it was important. I accepted Christ as my Savior."

We all need to have a sense that God has placed us on earth for a reason, Weir says, and those who are aging or dying are no exception.

Paul Brand, the missionary doctor and coauthor with Philip Yancey of *Fearfully and Wonderfully Made,* writes of his own mother's sense of purpose long after her mission board said it was time to retire. At age sixty-nine, her mission board said it was time to come home after years in India. And she was ready to, until she discovered another mountain range full of people who had never heard of Jesus. For the next twenty-six years, as she aged and began to die, Brand writes,

> Without mission society support, she climbed those mountains, built a little wooden shack, and worked another 26 years. Because of a broken hip and creeping paralysis, she could only walk with the aid of two bamboo sticks, but on the back of an old horse she rode all over the mountains, a medicine box strapped behind her. She sought out the unwanted and unlovely, the sick, the maimed, and the blind, and brought treatment to them.

When Granny Brand died at the age of ninety-five, she left a legacy of lives touched by the gospel. The last time he saw her in

India before she died, Brand remembers his mother, sitting surrounded by townspeople as she shared with them about Jesus. "Granny's own rheumy eyes are shining, and standing beside her I can see what she must be seeing through failing eyes: intent faces gazing with absolute trust and affection on one they have grown to love."[10] Indeed, God still has significant plans for our lives as we grow old and approach our deaths.

RECEIVING THE ELDERLY

The difference between the community that learns to approach death together and the community that doesn't is striking. Dunlop, the geriatrician, recalls two patients who died just days apart. One died of a cerebral hemorrhage, and Dunlop left the patient's room to give the man's wife the bad news. He was gladly surprised to discover "a group of Christian friends praying for him and supporting her." The spouse of another patient who died that week offered a disturbing contrast—what we miss without a church community. When Dunlop told the husband of one of his patients that his wife died, Dunlop says, "his first response was, 'Now who will take care of me?'"

Ministry to the elderly and their families must not be a specialty for only some interested folks within the church. Not everyone who dies grows old. Though we may expect to live to a ripe old age, nothing guarantees it. Younger people die in car accidents, while cancer or heart disease frequently strikes those who are middle aged. We all need to learn to die well, whatever age we are. Our lives will be enriched by thoughtfully and prayerfully considering our death.

That is why ministry to the elderly "must cross generational lines," Dunlop says. "All believers should be taught the lessons of Job, the comfort of the Psalms and the promise of the resurrection before times of difficulty come. The church needs to foster deep relationships within itself that will be sustaining at the end of life."[12]

Serving the elderly can help us confront our own mortality, another reason why their presence in the church is important to the rest of the congregation. As they decline, the elderly may slow down physically and mentally. Their needs are various and often complicated. The old and sick may simply be difficult to watch. I remember having difficulty visiting a hospice Alzheimer's patient during meal times. The smell of the institutional food and mixed nutritional drinks combined with very sloppy eating was often difficult for me. But my presence recognized the sacredness of this person with dementia, and it taught me not to be too confident and haughty in my own temporary health. The elderly and dying reflect our own future selves. That is perhaps the hardest task of caring for an old person, the inner undertaking of accepting our own limitations.

A congregation who does this well has a tremendous outreach opportunity. As the ranks of elderly and dying grow and the availability of family to care for them shrinks, there is a great need. Those who may have rejected the church in the past may be more open to the gospel if they're visited in the nursing home or a church offers support for them. Their families may also be more receptive to the gospel when their loved ones are receiving loving care from strangers. Indeed, this was the model of church growth for the early church. Care for the sick and dying attracted millions into the new Christian community, and the time is ready for Christians to offer the same love and care today.

But this can only be done by Christians who are able to confront their own deaths. "As long as we think that caring means only being nice and friendly to old people," write Henri Nouwen and Walter Gaffney, "we are apt to forget how much more important it is for us to be willing and able to be present to those we care for. And how can we be fully present to the elderly when we are hiding from our own aging?"[13] Nouwen, who gave up an academic career at Harvard in order to care for elderly and disabled people, says we must receive the dying person we are becoming.[14] "Only he who has recognized the relativity of his own life can bring a smile to the face of a man who feels the closeness of death."[15]

A CULTURE OF RESURRECTION

A congregation that does these things will more fully embody the gospel of Jesus Christ. Throughout the Bible we see a pattern of death bringing forth life. In Genesis after Adam and Eve fall and bring death into the world, God promised them that he would send a Savior.

The theme of death and resurrection continues. The Israelites walked through the separated waters of the Red Sea. Fleeing the Egyptian army, they walked through death and into life toward the Promised Land. Jesus said that a seed must fall into the ground and die before it bears fruit. Jesus himself died and rose again. And Paul wrote, "I die every day" (1 Corinthians 15:31).

The church embodies this reality of life following death. The Christian life is full of joy and hope not because Jesus makes us smiley with upbeat attitudes. But we enjoy an abiding hope that the God who brings life to the dead will do the same for us—not only in the last day but this one too. This deep hope pervades everything done by the congregation and individual believers. And when it is expressed in daily activities—faith that a difficult job situation will yield spiritual fruit or perseverance in the long-term care of a parent—it embodies a culture of resurrection. Churches can teach this culture and let it flourish in the care for the dying.

A culture of resurrection takes the lessons of dying well and the hope of new life in Christ and applies them throughout the life of the Christian and in the body of the church.

In the church, Christians learn about and become saturated by the gospel. The gospel, put one way, is that through the Holy Spirit we have the life of Jesus, given by the Father. This life is stronger than death, which because of our sin and separation from God would otherwise be our due. We begin expressing the life of God at our salvation and continue to do so in greater and greater faithfulness throughout eternity.

The church is where we learn what it means to be a Christian, in Sunday school and sermons and small group fellowships, where we hear the stories of the Bible and understand their meaning. However, we learn and apply those lessons best not just when we hear them taught but when we see and live them. When we worship God in our funerals and rejoice during baptisms. When we celebrate at weddings and support one another during our weaker moments. When we meet together week after week, when we care for the poor and when we introduce those unfamiliar with the life of God to its bounteous riches, we live out the culture of resurrection.

In these everyday moments we educate ourselves on how to live life walking in the Spirit, communing with God. We learn its meaning, not through words but through actions. As we all grow older, these events and activities are signposts marking the passage of life; they allow us to measure where we are in relation to where we should be. If we cannot learn to die well (to live our final days reconciled with those we leave behind and anticipating our future life with God), we cannot learn to live well. Churches that are "growing younger" don't allow their members to do what they all must: grow older.

Caregivers will find their loads lighter, and the elderly will find the challenges of growing old less burdensome when the church lives out of a culture not of youth but of resurrection. We understand that death leads to life, and we're more willing to pick up one another's burdens, whether providing respite care or a weekday lunch to a woman caring for an elderly parent or visiting an old man on his deathbed.

Churchwide care for the elderly and the activities we perform when death occurs are important for two basic reasons. As Christians do these things and see them done, we make small preparations, minor adjustments over time, toward a life with God. And second, Christians know what to do, how to behave, when these challenging circumstances arrive in our own lives. When we witness friends aging well or caring well for their elderly, it provides a model for us to follow. We won't need to figure everything out for the first time when our turn comes.

Care for the elderly and dying forms a congregation in ways youth work cannot. When we provide a ride to a homebound person or regularly visit the nursing home, it helps us all to recognize life's limits. Perhaps most of us or our loved ones will grow old before we die, and we should be prepared to meet those unique challenges. However, care for the elderly is an important spiritual discipline for everyone, because death is in all our futures. Caring for an elder will help us face death whenever it meets us and life more faithfully in every area of our lives.

When we allow ourselves to be confronted by death, our little excuses for unfaithfulness fall away. And we are prodded toward living more in view of what's truly important. In my own life, I'm learning to take more joy in and more care to develop those things that have the most significance. My three kids, my wife, my family and my friends—the quality of these relationships will be the measure of my life. And while I worry about my career and stress about being a provider and wonder what God has called me to in this part of my life, I know that God will bring life—whether or not I can envision what that will be today—out of my concerns. And I know that God will create meaning and goodness through my relationships with my family and those he has put around me.

THE CHURCH AND THE TRAJECTORY OF LIFE

"Our church doesn't have enough funerals," associate pastor John Stoltzfus said in his annual All Saints' Day sermon. In his suburban Mennonite congregation, members tend to move away from the area after they retire. They move into denominational retirement communities, or they head south to warmer climates. Sometimes, older members will continue to spend their summers in the Chicago area but winter somewhere in the Sun Belt. So, in his eight years as senior pastor Todd Friesen has performed just ten funerals. Other pastors he knows, who serve at churches to which members retire, perform on average one funeral a week.

Such a lack of funerals, Todd Friesen says, are a missed opportunity for spiritual formation. A funeral, he says, is like the North Star to a sailor. By comparing his or her position in the sea to that of the North Star in the sky, a navigator knows where the ship is and how to adjust its direction to get to the destination. At a funeral, "you get these coordinates" to position yourself in life says Friesen.

Though Friesen has performed fewer funerals than other pastors, he's done enough to know how family and friends measure the life of the deceased. The two commandments of Christ, to love God and love your neighbor, are all we talk about at funerals. "No one's going to ask what pay grade you had at your job, and was it an associate or assistant position. Nobody cares. It's the love of God, and it's the love of neighbor, and the way that this person helped me to connect with God and my neighbor that is or isn't her legacy," he says. Of course, right now we care, but that's why funerals are so helpful on life's journey. In contrast, at funerals we remember and celebrate when people helped us to know God and be neighbors.

Funerals are opportunities to measure ourselves by the same stick we're measuring others. "He was a good dad," we say, "and a loving husband." Or, "She took care of the people who worked for her, and she mentored other young women in church." When we say that about another, we also ask the same questions of ourselves.

Funerals help us to measure our days. For me, this means looking at my place in the continuum of life. Approaching middle age, my life is not full of opportunity and potential in the way it was when I was twenty-five. With children, a mortgage and a career, my life is circumscribed in ways I sometimes find frustrating. But measuring my days teaches me that I still can make audacious plans for my life. I am refocused and reoriented.

I realize again what a precious time of life I enjoy now. At a funeral earlier this year, I saw children, grandchildren and great-grandchildren, plus a number of friends gathered around the grave of a beloved old man. While we mourned, we also appreciated what he brought to the world, and that was most directly seen in his family. Measuring my days at the graveside, I saw that what he had completed so beautifully, I have only just begun. Tears came to my eyes as I watched my daughter lift a rose and, with the seriousness only a three-year-old can offer, place it on his coffin.

Friesen's church helps the congregation reflect on life's continuum by marking significant points in member's lives. At every stage in life the church offers ministries, relationships and services. But for significant milestones the church combines a service or ritual with a gift or other tangible marker. At a birth or adoption the baby is dedicated during the service and a red rose is placed on the pulpit. Beginning in third grade, children have presentations during worship, and at the first, they receive a Bible with inscriptions from members of the church. At twelve, children receive a mentor, an adult member of the church who is a nonparental source of guidance, wisdom and companionship. This also creates valuable intergenerational relationships. The church marks other milestones when a young person makes the decision to become a Christian, when someone joins the church as a member, at high school graduation, marriage, mission trips and retirement.

At death a member is remembered in a funeral, and again on All Saints' Day. Throughout the year a plaque hangs on a wall in the sanctuary, inscribed with the names of members who have passed away. Every year, on the All Saints' Day service the church remembers those who have died that year. A young person stands beside the plaque and reads aloud the new names that have been added that year, members who have now joined the eternal communion of saints.

While these are official markers, the church has other ways of fostering a vision for life with God throughout life's stages. The testimonies of church members provide a chance for individuals to reflect on their own lives and share that with the congregation. "People at various stages of life give us a vision for our own life at that stage," says Friesen. After Friesen's own grandmother died, at age ninety-nine, he was particularly struck by the usefulness of testimonies from older members. "My grandmother's influence on me started when she was eighty-nine and extended to ninety-nine. In the eyes of our culture, she's a useless person. But her most productive time in my life was her final ten years." This is something that everyone approaching or in retirement needs to hear, Friesen says. "You think nobody's paying attention" because of your age. "Think again. You can have a tremendous impact on people in your final decades. And you're going to have more of them than you think." A major job for the church, Friesen says, is to "give people a vision for the good life in the seasons of fall and winter."

On occasion, the congregation takes a look at itself during a service. Once, a worship leader asked groups of people to stand according to age, while the rest of the church applauded or otherwise recognized the group at this place in life. As the age groups grew older, fewer and fewer people stood up. When finally the oldest members of the church were standing and had been recognized, the worship leader then asked the children to stand again. As the congregation looked at the oldest and youngest among them, all could see clearly the link between the two groups as the oldest, who have spent a lifetime as caretakers of the church, pass on their work and their faith to those two or three generations younger.

"At each step in life, we're trying to give this sense of the with-God life," Friesen says. And when that life nears its end, its posture toward God has never really changed. "God is still with us," as he has been throughout our lives, "right to our final breath."

ETERNAL PRESENCE

Finally, the church builds a culture of resurrection when it fosters a sense of the universal body of Christ, across geography and through time. Those who have died are still present with us as members of the body of Christ. Death has not severed that spiritual relationship. All is not over at our final breath, neither for the dead nor those still alive. The dead, of course, go on to a greater and fuller life with God. Those still alive, however, are not entirely severed from the great body of Christians no longer walking the earth, though our churches have largely forgotten our brothers and sisters "asleep in Christ."

Old church buildings and those Christian communities that maintain their centuries-old traditions provide a stark contrast with modern churches in how they remember—even live among—their dead brothers and sisters. Until the nineteenth century, church buildings were often graveyards, with walls and floors holding the bones of those who worshiped in ages past. Walking into such a church today may seem creepy or morbid at first, but from a spiritual perspective these gatherings of the faithful are alive with the prayers, the history, the culture, the faith of generations.

The converted Orthodox poet Scott Cairns writes of his discovery of the Orthodox attitude toward the dead, which more closely resembles that of Christians from nearly any era but the modern. "For starters," he says, "the dead are unlikely to be spoken of as dead. They are asleep. Since the resurrection, Christian people do not die per se. They fall asleep. They are said to have fallen asleep in the Lord."[16]

Cairns was at first disturbed by the Orthodox practice of burying without embalming, out of respect for the integrity of the body. Orthodox funeral services include open caskets with the dead body in full view. "I was initially startled," he says, "then strangely moved."[17] While our culture hides from death, Cairns's congregation was comfortable, unafraid and welcoming.

"Throughout the liturgy that followed, family and friends continued to worship by [the deceased's] side. Children and adults both turned to him throughout the service, as if to see if he was comfortable, attending to him as if he were still present."

Comparing this loving and respectful attitude to the death of his own father, Cairns writes, "We missed out on most of this." After a two-day struggle in which his father struggled just to breathe, the ordeal finally ended. "We wept, of course, but we had little in our experience to help us attend as fully to his body . . . as we might have or as, perhaps, we should have."[18]

And the Orthodox maintain their reverent attitude toward the dead long after anyone alive remembers who they are. In the monasteries of Mount Athos, Cairns writes of basements full of bones, and of monks who proudly call them "my brothers." Indeed they are. The living Christians and the dead are still of one body, still of one hope.

Christians challenge the modern idea that death is a solitary event. Those who are a part of the body of Christ are never separated. Theologian Therese Lysaught writes,

> Christians do not die alone. Rather, death within the Christian tradition is an experience of ongoing, communal presence. Again and again in these rites, a world in which the living remember, accompany, and care for the dead is concretely rendered. Through a continuous set of rites and practices, the church maintains a constant and unbroken presence to those who are dying beyond the point of their burial.[19]

Though churches these days are likely to run into building codes that prevent them from tearing into the drywall to bury members, some churches have found alternative ways of caring for their "sleeping" members. One I visited had a garden outside the building and a marble wall rising beside the church. Walking through the garden, church members could see the names, carved into the wall, where the cremated ashes of church members remained. Some had names, but no dates. The future occupant had yet to be called to join her deceased brothers and sisters. These columbaria, a place where the ashes of the dead are stored, offer strangers a sense of the continuity of the faith and a reminder of our own destination. It is a visible reminder of the culture of resurrection.

The columbaria also offers church members basic help as they grieve. They have the opportunity to prepare for the place where their bodies will await the second coming and the resurrection of the dead. And they allow loved ones to visit the resting places of their beloved any day of the week, but at least every Sunday.

Such reminders offer an occasion to remember who we are as part of a far larger body of Christians that extends two thousand years. As much as science, medicine and a rapidly changing society have altered things and imposed new challenges and difficult questions, life and death are still the same. People who "are up-to-date on their forgiveness," as Friesen says, who have not accumulated baggage to burden them at the end of life, these people tend to die well. People who have loved God and are at peace with him and their neighbors don't need last minute instructions on dying well. The church, by teaching and living out the values of a life lived with a view to the resurrection, expresses a culture of resurrection. Such a culture cares for its elderly and their caregivers. It also teaches young and old to live and die well.

As medicine allows us to live longer while ill, even terminally ill, we have more time to make these preparations. We have time to offer forgiveness and tell others "I'm sorry." We have time to turn to God and devote ourselves more fully to him. Yet, while a medical diagnosis may provide more urgency and less time to reconcile with others, the basic actions of offering apologies and turning to God are no different near death than at any other time in life.

We prepare for death and we see the Christian life in practice by providing a means for the dying to continue their presence in the church. Not only does it offer an opportunity for the dying and elderly to continue to fulfill the ministry to which God has called them, but the rest of the congregation sees life lived and ended with hope and faithfulness.

11

LIVING IN
LIGHT OF DEATH

J OYCE TOMPKINS WAS JUST FOUR YEARS OLD WHEN her great-aunt
came to live with the family. "She was blind," Joyce told me, "and
I ended up staying in a room with her and reading the Bible to her."
Sharing a bedroom with a sixty-year-old woman was a wonderful
opportunity, as Joyce remembers. Over the next fourteen years,
Joyce and her aunt shared that bedroom. It was a family value—to
care for all in need. "On both sides of our family," Joyce explains,
"we have people who cared about other people. It was just a matter
of that's what they did; they helped people."

Those early experiences of caring, even in small ways, for elderly family members were invaluable when her own parents
needed to be cared for. "When my father would say, 'Help people because you never know who might have to give you a drink
of water,' he had no idea he was going to have a stroke and be
paralyzed on one side."

After high school, Joyce started working but eventually decided to enroll in college. She didn't enjoy her job and wanted
something different. But just when her work experience and col-

lege degree could have launched her in a new direction, Joyce's
father had a stroke. "He was diabetic," she says, "and two years
before his stroke he had a heart attack." Now, at seventy-four, he
couldn't get himself a glass of water.

He had served in three wars, World War II, Korea and Vietnam, and he ended his service without a wound. In the hospital,
after decades of caring for his family and serving his country,
Joyce was shocked by the doctor's assumption that her father
would go to a nursing home. "One of the first things that came
out of the doctor's mouth," Joyce says, was "we have a list of
nursing homes we can take him to." The family would care for
him, she told the doctor, just as he had cared for others.

Three years later, while Joyce was helping to care for her father, her mother was diagnosed with breast cancer. With the aid
of professional nurses and community support during the day,
Joyce was able to care for both her parents for the next two years,
until her father died.

As her mother recovered and became able to care for herself
and her father passed away, Joyce moved from Kansas City to
Chicago to study theology. Finally, Joyce thought, she would
transition to a career she loved. Six months later, her mother's
health suddenly declined. Her sister then moved in to care for
their mother, and Joyce began commuting between Chicago and
Kansas City. She took classes half the week, and took care of her
mother the other half.

It wasn't an easy decision to begin such a grueling schedule. But
her sister, who worked nights, needed a break. I need to do what I
need to do, Joyce told herself. "If it meant me leaving school, then
that's what was going to happen, because Mom actually voiced the
fact that she did not want to go into a nursing home." Joyce told her
mother that we never know what may become necessary, but that

if the family could take care of her, they would.

From when her father first had a stroke till her mother's eventual death from breast cancer, Joyce spent a decade caring for her parents, and her experiences led her to help others who were caring for their own family. Through it all, Joyce sees God's hand.

When I look back at what God's done in my life, I will always say that I'm grateful for that window of time. I don't know what his whole purpose was for me being here, but if he used the first years of my life to prepare me for those ten years and if he would have said to me the next day I'm ready for you to go, I would have been okay. If that's what you had me here for was to walk with them through their deaths, that in itself would be great.

When she graduates from her program, Joyce says, "I want to work with senior citizens. They need something to do," she says, and it's simple for the church to provide that. "They have a wealth of knowledge," Tompkins says, and she sees an opportunity to direct those gifts into the life of the church.

Her experience with her parents has shown Joyce that "there is a great need for people to come in and show compassion." She says, "I've been in the hospital many a time in the emergency room with my parents, and I'll see an elderly person in the bed in the emergency room and then there's that feeble husband or wife with them, no one else." What happens when a spouse dies, Tompkins asks. "What about that person who doesn't have a support system? Who helps them? Maybe all their friends are gone now." If Tompkins is available, she says, at least they know someone will be there.

Like many women caring for elderly parents, Joyce's life has been formed by death. She made significant sacrifices in her time, career and personal relationships to care for both of her parents. Yet she's found meaning in that work, so much so that she plans to continue it as God's calling for the next part of her life.

Death ought to form how we live our lives because the qualities that define a good life are those that make up a good death. When we allow ourselves to be confronted by death, it is not easy. It's tough to recognize that our lives on this earth will end, and it can be hard to realize that much of what we pursue in life has little ultimate meaning. In response we may deploy a range of methods to avoid being confronted by death. We zealously seek medical treatment to forestall the inevitable or we simply maintain lives that are too busy to be interrupted by a trip to the nursing home. Whatever method we pursue, avoiding death often means refusing to recognize what is valuable in our own lives. We can work against this tendency in a number of ways.

INTRODUCING THE YOUNG TO THE OLD

Joyce found it natural to put aside some personal goals in order to care for her parents; it came as a result of her upbringing. She was introduced to the elderly and even the dying from a young age. She grew up with a blind elderly aunt sharing her bedroom. Personally I've learned to be intentional with my own children about creating opportunities for them to interact with the elderly. Going to dinner at great-grandma's assisted living home is a wonderful opportunity to introduce them to a group of elderly residents. We eat dinner, and great-grandma's friends stop by to say hello. Afterward we all sit outside and watch the kids play in puddles. Something beautiful happens when the old and young interact, though there is nothing particularly special about a single visit or dinner. It is in these casual interactions that our children can learn to value the elderly, treasure time with them, and learn practical ways to care for them as they age and face death.

Our family has taken this another step, and when choosing a church, we've sought out an intergenerational congregation. It's certainly tempting to go to a church that attracts mostly people our age. Such churches are an easy fit—lots of people our age to befriend and lots of programs for kids our children's age. Yet an intergenerational congregation allows our children exposure to the whole continuum of life. Together as a community of faith, we bless infants, celebrate marriages and mourn deaths. If our children never attend a funeral until they are in middle age, have we really equipped them to deal with death's realities? If we are to change how our culture and the church view death and the dying, we must first start at home.

FAMILY RELATIONSHIPS

Despite her evident care and respect for the elderly, on two occasions Joyce Tompkins had reasonable excuses to be unable to care for her parents. When her father had a stroke, she had just graduated from college and was ready to pursue a new career. By the time her mother became ill, Joyce lived hundreds of miles away and was in graduate school. The expense of commuting home every week and paying tuition must have been a significant burden. Yet she placed a priority on caring for her family and taking up the responsibility that Joyce's parents had taught her was hers. "You never know when you're going to need a drink of water," she says.

Often in our culture, it is necessary to move away from family in order to pursue a career. Whether a company moves its offices, a local industry closes or educational opportunities are elsewhere, we are a mobile people. While we move from place to place, we also must recognize the duties that are still ours. While Joyce's commitment to caring for her mother didn't mean that she stopped her studies, it did mean hopping on a plane every week. Cultivating close family relationships means recognizing and accepting the extra work that will be required of us when we live far away. For others, it may mean taking extra vacation time to maintain relationships with family or care for relatives. Whether we live down the street or across the country from our loved ones, we must be willing and prepared to assist them when they need our care.

SUPPORT SYSTEMS

In the midst of a caregiving situation it's easy to become overwhelmed with the weight of responsibility, particularly if we are the only ones nearby to do the everyday work. Managing finances, schedules, doctors' appointments and medications can be a wearying full-time job. Joyce received help and provided help to her sister, who for a while cared for her mother in Kansas City while Joyce studied theology near Chicago. As we look to care for those who are dying, we must acknowledge our need for community support, those people in our circles who can provide respite, encouragement and assistance as we care for our loved ones.

While we often use the more clinical term support systems, these are simply relationships. The relationships we have with family, friends, church members and colleagues are what will help us through our own deaths or help us care for those we love. It takes some humility to recognize that we need help in life. For me it took a confrontation with death—in hospice and on staff at a funeral home—to be able to recognize that these relationships are not just important because I enjoy them but because I depend on them.

FINAL WISHES

A friend of mine who works in intensive care told me recently how difficult it is to decide how to provide medical care to someone who isn't able to provide any guidance to a preferred method of treatment. For her it means that, to be on the safe side, they provide all the care the hospital has to offer. Still, it is often troubling when that care can be painful, invasive and seemingly futile.

Beyond particular medical issues, it's important to know how our loved ones want us to care for them. Joyce's mother had told her she didn't want to go to a nursing home. While Joyce said she couldn't guarantee that, she did offer to do her best to care for her mother in her own home. These conversations are vital to providing a foundation for a good death. As we encourage loved ones to talk frankly with us (and as we do this ourselves), we not only are assisting the caregivers but we are confronting our mortality in a way that can be instructive and deeply spiritual.

It's important to be able to tell others how we want to be cared for. It took me some time to realize that even as a younger, healthy man, I needed to do this. After spending four years researching and writing about dying well, I still have trouble recognizing my own mortality. Our desire to avoid thinking about our own death can prevent us from saying the important things to other people that will help us die well.

LOOK TO GOD

Despite all the sacrifices that Joyce undertook as she cared for her parents for the better part of a decade, she was able to see God's hand at work. I've spoken to many caregivers who have found the privilege of caring for someone who is dying to be one of the most precious gifts of God. After ten years caring for her parents, with her career and aspirations on hold, Joyce was able to say that she was even ready for God to take her home.

That may be the most wonderful aspect of the art of dying. There is beauty and blessing in being with someone as she moves from this world to the next. As we attend to another believer whose soul is returning to God, we capture a glimpse of the beautiful destiny that awaits us. We are reminded of our need for him. We are spurred on to live with eternity in view, knowing that it is our living well that will define our death.

My most recent hospice patient was a ninety-two-year-old man named Gene. He had cancer and heart disease, but I visited him and sometimes his wife every week. We talked and got to know one another. His great-grandson, it turned out, worked in the same field as I did. So Gene and I talked about the publishing industry, we prayed together, and I read him Scripture. Over Christmas, before I left to visit relatives, I read Gene the incarnation story from Luke.

Gene's body was falling apart. Literally, his tooth fell out one night before I visited. And cancer ravaged his organs. I began seeing Gene with the knowledge that he would soon die. As the months went on, he spent more and more time asleep. Still I visited, as he lay in bed or sat in his chair, and I prayed for him, knowing that his time was soon to come.

I was devastated the day I found out Gene had passed away. I missed the message from hospice, and I showed up at Gene's nursing home room. It was empty. As I returned to the hallway the nursing-home staff told me he'd died. I fought back tears, and as soon as I found out the details I headed back to my car, sad yet grateful for the months he and I chatted on Saturday afternoons.

Dying is an art only because through it God is at work. Only in God's hand can something ugly and terrible be transformed into a thing of beauty and purpose. In the end death is as mysterious to us as resurrection. In our churches we spiritually enter into Christ's death and resurrection in the waters of baptism. In the same way, we must practice for our deaths, prepare to care for others as they face it and look for the hand of God who welcomes us through death to life everlasting.

STUDY GUIDE

Questions for Personal Reflection or Group Discussion

CHAPTER 1: WHEN DEATH ARRIVES

1. What is your personal experience with death? Have you ever had sustained, face-to-face engagement with someone who was dying?
2. How do you think our culture deals with death? Would things be better if our cultural response was different?
3. Do you consider yourself familiar with death or end-of-life issues?
4. Is there such a thing as a good death?
5. What should be different when a Christian dies as opposed to a non-Christian?
6. How should Christian ethics apply at the end of life?
7. Is death ever a good thing?

CHAPTER 2: GRADUAL DYING AND END-OF-LIFE CARE

1. How have you experienced gradual dying or caregiving for a dying loved one among family or friends?
2. What are the positive and negative aspects of gradual dying?
3. Would you personally want to have advance notice about your death, or would you rather not know?
4. How might you live differently if you knew you would die within the next three years?
5. How do you balance the desire to use medicine to fight off disease with the need to accept death?

6. Does being pro-life make some Christians anti-death?
7. Have you thought about what you want for your end-of-life care?

CHAPTER 3: LOSING THE CHRISTIAN DEATH

1. What do you think are elements of a good death, of a Christian death?
2. Should today's Christians think about death in the same way as Christians of past centuries? Did they think about death too much or in odd ways? Should modern Christians come up with their own attitude about dying?
3. Should dying be seen more as a spiritual event?
4. Have you ever witnessed a death? Did you find it spiritually meaningful?
5. What do you think about angels, Jesus or deceased loved ones visiting someone who is dying? Are these stories true, or do they strictly occur in the minds of those who are dying?
6. How does Jesus' resurrection affect how Christians think about and practice their dying?

CHAPTER 4: THE INDIVIDUAL, THE CHURCH AND *ARS MORIENDI*

1. Would you want to hear a sermon like John Donne's "Death's Duel"?
2. Should there be such a thing as an *ars moriendi* today?
3. How can Jesus be an example to us in dying?
4. Do you fear death, and does your faith offer you comfort?
5. What might it take for you to "to joyfully and confidently embark on the path toward God" in your death, as Martin Luther writes?
6. Do you see dying as something actively undertaken, or simply something that happens because of illness or natural causes?
7. Whether a funeral, memorial service or other event, what is the best way to mark someone's death?

CHAPTER 5: THE SPIRITUALITY OF DYING

1. What happens, spiritually speaking, when someone dies?
2. Is it right to expect or hope for evidence of a spiritual nature at the end of life? Should it be seen as a window to the next world?

3. If spiritual experiences at the end of life are normal and natural, should that affect the medical decisions we make?

4. Jim Harrell experienced a profound change in his relationship with God and his understanding of his purpose in the time he had left. What changes would you want to make in your life if you were in the same position?

5. What hardship have you faced that, while tremendously difficult, turned out for good. Would you choose that hardship again because of the result it produced?

6. How do you need to be prepared spiritually in order to enter life with God?

CHAPTER 6: THE HARDEST CONVERSATION YOU'LL EVER HAVE

1. Have you ever had an end-of-life conversation with someone?

2. Have you ever told anyone your end-of-life wishes?

3. What concerns do you have about the end of your life? What are your biggest fears? What issue do you need to have resolved?

4. What do you want your last days to look like?

CHAPTER 7: CARING FOR THE DYING

1. Have you ever been the main person providing care to someone else?

2. What challenges did you face as a caregiver? What did you gain from the experience?

3. Do you see a connection between the Christian doctrine of the incarnation and the sacredness of the body and providing physical care for someone?

4. Do you feel squeamish about being with someone who is dying?

5. Outside of being a caregiver for someone, how can you learn to be someone who brings "a spirit of peace," as Dallas Willard says, into someone's life?

6. To whom do you need to say "Please forgive me," "I forgive you," "Thank you" or "I love you"?

7. Has someone's role as a caregiver caused conflict in your family? Have you resolved those issues?

CHAPTER 8: THE CHRISTIAN FUNERAL

1. How do the funerals that you have attended reflect beliefs about life and death?

2. What beliefs should a Christian funeral reflect?

3. How does a funeral shape the way that someone mourns for a loved one?

4. Is a funeral an essential part of mourning, or is it simply one way of many in which people can express their grief?

5. How does the gospel story fit into the way the story is told of a Christian's life in a funeral?

6. What is the difference between a Christian funeral service and a memorial?

CHAPTER 9: GRIEF AND MOURNING

1. A half century ago, C. S. Lewis wrote, "I'm aware of being an embarrassment to everyone I meet." Do you think the bereaved might still say the same thing today?

2. How long do you think it should take someone to recover from the death of a loved one? At what point might someone be through grieving?

3. Do you think that older ways of formalized communally expressed grief (when people wore black or special jewelry to signal they were "in mourning") would be a good thing to begin doing once again?

4. What do you think about the Jewish mourning rituals?

5. Is it right to talk about grieving in terms of "tasks" or "a job" to do?

6. If Christians are not supposed to mourn "as those who have no hope," how should they mourn?

7. How should a Christian balance hope in a future eternal life with God with present grief?

8. Walter Wangerin says that it is through sorrow that Christians discover joy. Has that been true in your life?

CHAPTER 10: A CULTURE OF RESURRECTION

1. Fred Smith said that he would like the words "He stretched others" written on his tombstone. What would you like said on yours?

2. How is the art of dying the same as the art of living?

3. How can people stay active and live meaningful lives into their elderly years?

4. Why is it important to maintain relationships and meaningful goals throughout life? How can the church play a role in helping elderly members do this?

5. In what ways do you see yourself living purposefully in your old age?

6. How might churches do a better job at helping elderly members stay integrated into the congregation and living with a biblical vision of their final years?

7. How do the church and individual Christians tangibly live out their belief in Jesus Christ's resurrection from the grave?

CHAPTER 11: LIVING IN LIGHT OF DEATH

1. Did you have experiences as a child living with a grandparent or elderly relative?

2. How can caring for a dying person or spending time with the elderly help people better live their lives?

3. Have you had to change your life plans in order to take care of a family member? How has that affected your life currently? Would you say, as Joyce does, "I'm grateful for that window of time"?

4. If you live a significant distance from family members, how has that affected the ways in which you maintain relationships and care for loved ones?

5. How have you seen God working in someone's life while they or a family member neared death?

6. Dying is nearly always a difficult, painful process. Does it make sense to talk about an "art" of dying?

ACKNOWLEDGMENTS

I HOPE *THE ART OF DYING* WILL BE of much help to individuals and families confronting death. If it is, a number of people deserve credit.

My parents, Bob and Ann, I wish to thank for doing what parents do, and doing it well. And a special thanks to my mom for asking me one winter day to visit my dying aunt. Her experiences as a caregiver and our conversations about it are reflected here.

My wife, Clarissa, has been a terrific editor and supporter, especially when I wanted to write a book about death. I had no idea when we got married that she'd be able to help me shape my unformed ideas into something coherent. If I had, I wouldn't have waited a full fourteen months from the day we met to get married. Her editing in nearly every stage of this project has been invaluable. I couldn't pay for better help. This book has been a presence in our lives for at least half of our marriage and through the birth of two of our children. Clarissa has been a wonderful supporter to me and this project, patient all those Saturdays and vacation days while I headed out to write and she watched the kids. Thanks, Clarissa, for being willing to allow me to pursue a dream that makes no practical sense.

The guys at Hultgren Funeral Home, Tim, Jeff, Scott and Darcy, showed me ministry to those in grief. During the year I worked there, their friendship, conversations, professionalism and caring hearts broke down all the stereotypes too common about funeral homes.

The editors at *Christianity Today* showed me how to write and gave me the chance to practice and learn. Many thanks to Ted (both a great editor and boss), Agnieszka, Collin, David, Madison, Mark, Stan and Tim. And thanks for the staff time I spent doing a lot of this reporting.

Doctors John Dunlop and David Fisher shared their work with me and displayed professional excellence and ministry to those at the end of their lives. Both allowed me to accompany them as they made the rounds through the nursing home. And John provided valuable feedback to the manuscript.

Thanks to Steven Weibley, who presided over a beautiful funeral service at the Carlisle Congregational Church in Massachusetts. Steven showed me the importance of a well-performed Christian funeral service, and he gave much-appreciated support in the later stages of drafting the manuscript. The congregation and Steven's pastoral care to my wife's grandparents also provided inspiration and an example in caring for the elderly at the end of life.

Thanks to all those who shared their stories with me. Their words are woven through this book, both where their stories are told and everywhere else.

Thanks to Kathleen Sanford and the rest of the staff and volunteers at CNS Home Health and Hospice, where I have volunteered the last few years. Their work is amazing, and I'm glad to be a part of it.

J. I. Packer originally encouraged me to pursue the idea that became this book. It's in a much different form than when I first discussed it with him, but I do hope he still thinks it was a good idea. Thanks to Dr. Packer for his encouragement.

Al Hsu took a chance on this book idea from a first-time book author. Thanks, Al, for believing in this book and my ability to write it. Thanks also for a fine job as editor.

NOTES

Chapter 1: When Death Arrives

[1]Stephen Kiernan, *Last Rights: Rescuing the End of Life from the Medical System* (New York: St. Martin's Press, 2006), p. 53.

[2]Virginia Morris, *Talking About Death* (Chapel Hill, N.C.: Algonquin Books, 2004), p. 61.

[3]Robert V. Wells, *Facing the "King of Terrors": Death and Society in an American Community, 1750-1990* (New York: Cambridge University Press, 2000), p. 195.

[4]William Colby, "How We Die in America," an excerpt of *Unplugged: Reclaiming our Right to Die in America* (New York: Amacom Books, 2006), AuthorViews.com <www.authorviews.com/authors/colby/obd.htm>.

[5]Philippe Aries, *The Hour of Our Death: The Classic History of Western Attitudes Toward Death Over the Last One Thousand Years* (New York: Barnes & Noble, 1981), p. 569.

[6]Sherwin B. Nuland, *How We Die* (New York: Vintage, 1995), p. 8.

[7]Interviews done by the author are not footnoted in this book. All research outside of first-person interviews, however, is footnoted.

[8]Nuland, *How We Die,* pp. 98-99.

[9]Kallistos Ware, "Go Joyfully: The Mystery of Death and Resurrection," in *The Inner Kingdom,* (Crestwood, N.Y.: St. Vladimir's Seminary Press, 2000), p. 30.

[10]Isaac the Syrian, quoted in ibid., p. 27.

Chapter 2: Gradual Dying and End-of-Life Care

[1]Joanne Lynn and David M. Adamson, "Living Well at the End of Life: Adapting Health Care to Serious Chronic Illness in Old Age," a RAND Corporation White Paper, 2003 <www.rand.org/pubs/white_papers/2005/WP137.pdf>.

[2]Ibid.

[3]Stephen Kiernan, *Last Rights* (New York: St. Martin's Press, 2006), p. 7.

[4]Ibid., p. 12.

[5]Ibid.

[6]Sherwin B. Nuland, *How We Die* (New York: Vintage, 1995), p. 142.

[7]Virginia Morris, *Talking About Death* (Chapel Hill, N.C.: Algonquin Books, 2004), p. 59.

[8]See researcher Michael Balboni's response to Mark Galli's "Man Up, Christians," at "More on the Christians/Aggressive Measures Study," ChristianityToday.com, March 27, 2009 <http://blog.christianitytoday.com/ctliveblog/archives/2009/03/more_on_the_chr.html>.

[9]Andrea C. Phelps et al., "Religious Coping and Use of Intensive Life-Prolonging Care Near Death in Patients With Advanced Cancer," *Journal of the American Medical Association* 301, no. 11 (2009) <http://jama.ama-assn.org/cgi/content/abstract/301/11/1140>.

[10]Karen Kaplan, "Aligning a Medical Treatment Plan with God's Plan: Faith Drives Some Patients to Fight, and Suffer More at the End," *Los Angeles Times,* March 18, 2009 <www.latimes.com/news/local/la-sci-faith18-2009mar18,0,2501786.story>.

[11]"Questions and Answers on the Will to Live," National Right to Life <www.nrlc.org/euthanasia/willtolive/QAWTL.html>.

[12]Kiernan, *Last Rites,* p. 132.

[13]Maurice Steinberg and Stuart J. Youngner, eds., *End-of-Life Decisions: A Psychosocial Perspective* (Washington, D.C., American Psychiatric, 1998), p. 122.

[14]William A. Knaus, "The Study to Understand Prognosis and Preferences for Outcomes and Risks of Treatments, SUPPORT," ICU Research Unit, George Washington University Medical Center, Washington, D.C., 1998.

[15]Kiernan, *Last Rites,* p. 24.

[16]Ibid., p. 27.

[17]Ibid., p. 128.

Chapter 3: Losing the Christian Death

[1]John Fanestil, *Mrs. Hunter's Happy Death: Lessons on Living from People Preparing to Die* (New York: Random House, 2006), p. 89.

[2]See Gary B. Ferngren, *Medicine and Health Care in Early Christianity* (Baltimore: Johns Hopkins University Press, 2009).

[3]Gary Laderman, *The Sacred Remains: American Attitudes Toward Death, 1799-1883* (New Haven, Conn.: Yale University Press, 1999), p. 63.

[4]Robert V. Wells, *Facing the "King of Terrors"* (New York: Cambridge University Press, 2000), p. 285.

[5]Sherwin B. Nuland, *How We Die* (New York: Vintage, 1995), p. 256.

[6]Donald Heinz, *The Last Passage: Recovering a Death of Our Own* (New York: Oxford University Press, 1998), p. 10.

[7]Philippe Aries, *The Hour of Our Death* (New York: Barnes & Noble, 1981), p. 471.

[8]Wells, *Facing the "King of Terrors,"* p. 47 (italics added).

[9]Walter Wangerin, "How Long Good Friends? How Long Since Our Last Communication?" available at <walterwangerinjr.org/new_web/pdf/ec/friends-can13.doc>.

[10]Kiernan, *Last Rites,* p. 71.

[11]John Fanestil, "Graveside Hope: A Passion for Funeral Ministry," *Christian Century,* March 6, 2007, p. 24.

Chapter 4: The Individual, the Church and *Ars Moriendi*

[1]Isaak Walton, "The Life of Dr. John Donne," Project Canterbury website, <www.anglican history.org/Walton/donne.html>.

[2]Ibid.

[3]Ibid.

[4]R. C. Bald, *John Donne: A Life* (New York: Oxford University Press, 1986), p. 527.

[5]Arthur E. Imhof, *Facing Death,* ed. Howard M. Spiro, Mary G. McCrea Curnen and Lee Palmer Wandel (New Haven, Conn.: Yale University Press, 1996), p. 116.

[6]Paul Binski, *Medieval Death: Ritual and Representation* (Ithaca, N.Y.: Cornell University Press, 1996), pp. 39-40.

[7]Jean-Charles Didier, *Death and the Christian,* trans. J. J. Hepburne-Scott (New York: Hawthorn Books, 1961), p. 18.

[8]John Fanestil, *Mrs. Hunter's Happy Death* (New York: Random House, 2006), p. 61.

[9]Jeremy Taylor, "To the Right Hon. and Noblest Lord Richard, Earl of Carbery, Etc., Etc.," *Holy Dying,* Christian Classics Ethereal Library <www.ccel.org/ccel/taylor/holy_dying.toc .html>.

[10]Fanestil, *Mrs. Hunter's Happy Death,* pp. 53, 147.

[11]Eamon Duffy, *The Stripping of the Altars: Traditional Religion in England 1400-1580* (New Haven, Conn.: Yale University Press, 1992), pp. 313-14.

[12]Austra Reinis, *Reforming the Art of Dying: The* Ars Moriendi *in the German Reformation* (1519-1528) (Surrey, U.K.: Ashgate, 2007), p. 1.

[13]Ibid., p. 51.

[14]Ibid., p. 59.

[15]Ibid., p. 47.

[16]Frederick S. Paxton, *Christianizing Death* (Ithaca, N.Y.: Cornell University Press, 1990), p. 45.

[17]Ibid., p. 156.

[18]Fanestil, *Mrs. Hunter's Happy Death,* pp. 88-89.

[19]Ibid., p. 89.

[20]Philippe Aries, *The Hour of Our Death* (New York: Barnes & Noble, 1981), pp. 18, 19.

[21]Paxton, *Christianizing Death,* pp. 196-97.

[22]Ibid.

[23]Aries, *Hour of Our Death,* pp. 559-60.

[24]Lisa Takeuchi Cullen, *Remember Me: A Lively Tour of the New American Way of Death* (New York: HarperCollins, 2006), p. 27.

[25]Donald Heinz, *The Last Passage* (New York: Oxford University Press, 1998), p. 127.

Chapter 6: The Hardest Conversation You'll Ever Have

[1]Nancy Keating et al., "Physician Factors Associated with Discussions About End-of-Life Care," *Cancer,* January 2010.

[2]Gilbert Meilaender, "I Want to Burden My Loved Ones," Lutheran Church–Missouri Synod, 1999 <www.lcms.org/graphics/assets/media/WRHC/181_I Want to Burden My Loved Ones .PDF>.

[3]John Dunlop, "Death and Dying," in *Dignity and Dying: A Christian Appraisal,* ed. John F. Kilner, Arlene B. Miller and Edmund D. Pellegrino (Grand Rapids: Eerdmans, 1996), pp. 39-40.

Chapter 7: Caring for the Dying

[1]Gary B. Ferngren, *Medicine and Health Care in Early Christianity* (Baltimore: Johns Hopkins University Press, 2009), p. 102.

[2]Ibid., p. 114.

[3]Ibid., p. 5.

[4]Liston O. Mills, "Pastoral Care of the Dying and the Bereaved," in *Perspectives on Death,* ed. Liston O. Mills (Nashville: Abingdon, 1969), p. 254.

[5]Ibid., p. 258.

[6]Arlene B. Miller, "A Nurse's Experience," in *Dignity and Dying: A Christian Appraisal,* ed. John F. Kilner, Arlene B. Miller and Edmund D. Pellegrino (Grand Rapids: Eerdmans, 1996), p. 13.

[7]Maggie Callanan and Patricia Kelley, *Final Gifts* (New York: Bantam, 1997), p. 33.

[8]Ira Byock, *Dying Well: The Prospect for Growth at the End of Life* (New York: Putnam/Riverhead, 1997), p. 31.

[9]Martha Twaddle, "Hospice Care," in *Dignity and Dying: A Christian Appraisal,* ed. John F. Kilner, Arlene B. Miller and Edmund D. Pellegrino (Grand Rapids: Eerdmans, 1996), p. 187.

[10]Callanan and Kelley, *Final Gifts,* p. 21

Chapter 8: The Christian Funeral

[1]Frederick S. Paxton, *Christianizing Death: The Creation of a Ritual Process in Early Medieval Europe* (Ithaca, N.Y.: Cornell University Press, 1990), p. 24.

[2]Ben Peays, "Fantasy Funerals and Other Designer Ways of Going Out in Style," in *Everyday Theology: How to Read Cultural Texts and Interpret Trends,* ed. Kevin J. Vanhoozer, Charles A. Anderson and Michael J. Sleasman (Grand Rapids: Baker Academic, 2007), p. 214.

[3]Gary Laderman, *The Sacred Remains* (New Haven, Conn.: Yale University Press, 1999), p. 45.

[4]Thomas G. Long, *Accompany Them with Singing: The Christian Funeral* (Louisville: Westminster John Knox Press, 2009), p. 16.

[5]John Leland, "It's My Funeral and I'll Serve Ice Cream if I Want To," *New York Times,* July 20, 2006 <www.nytimes.com/2006/07/20/fashion/20funeral.html>.

[6]Ibid.

[7]Peays, "Fantasy Funerals," p. 214.

Chapter 9: Grief and Mourning

[1]C. S. Lewis, *A Grief Observed* (New York: Bantam Books, 1976), p. 10

[2]Philippe Aries, *The Hour of Our Death* (New York: Barnes & Noble, 1981), p. 576.

[3]Lewis, *Grief Observed,* p. 11.

[4]LaVonne Neff, "Three Women Out of Four: How the Church Can Meet the Needs of Its Widows," *Christianity Today,* November 8, 1985, p. 30.

[5]Paul K. Maciejewski et al., "An Empirical Examination of the Stage Theory of Grief," *Journal of the American Medical Association,* February 21, 2007.

[6]J. I. Packer, *A Grief Sanctified: Passing Through Grief to Peace and Joy* (Ann Arbor, Mich.: Servant Publications, 1997), p. 163.

[7]Jack Riemer, *Jewish Insights on Death and Mourning* (New York: Schocken, 1996), p. 12.

[8]Ibid., p. 14.

[9]Lewis, *Grief Observed,* p. 167.

[10]Walter Wangerin Jr., *Mourning into Dancing* (Grand Rapids: Zondervan, 1992), p. 26.

[11]Ibid., pp. 28-29.

[12]Ibid., p. 145.

Chapter 10: A Culture of Resurrection

[1]Introduction to "Justification Narrative," National Institute on Aging, U.S. National Institutes of Health, August 6, 2009 <www.nia.nih.gov/AboutNIA/BudgetRequests/FY2005/JustificationNarrative.htm>.

[2]"Caregiving in the U.S.," <www.caregiving.org/data/04execsumm.pdf>, accessed January 1, 2010.

[3]Donald H. Kausler, Barry C. Kausler and Jill A. Krupsaw, *The Essential Guide to Aging in the Twenty-First Century: Mind, Body, and Behavior* (Columbia: University of Missouri Press, 2007), p. 256.

[4]Ibid., p. 32.

[5]Ian S. Knox, *Older People and the Church* (London: T & T Clark, 2002), p. 112.

[6]Ibid., p. 117.

[7]Ibid., p. 232.

[8]Ibid., p. 106.

[9]Stanley Hauerwas, Carole Bailey Stoneking, Keith G. Meador and David Cloutier, eds., *Growing Old in Christ* (Grand Rapids: Eerdmans, 2003), p. 32

[10]Rowan Greer, "Special Gift and Special Burden: Views of Old Age in the Early Church," in ibid., pp. 37, 176.

[11]Paul Brand and Philip Yancey, *In His Image* (Grand Rapids: Zondervan, 1984), p. 46.

[12]John Dunlop, "Death and Dying," in *Dignity and Dying: A Christian Appraisal,* ed. John F. Kilner, Arlene B. Miller and Edmund D. Pellegrino (Grand Rapids: Eerdmans, 1996), p. 42.

[13]Henri J. M. Nouwen and Walter J. Gaffney, *Aging: The Fulfillment of Life* (New York: Doubleday, 1976), pp. 97- 98.

[14]Ibid., p. 101.

[15]Ibid., p. 102.

[16]Scott Cairns, *Short Trip to the Edge: Where Earth Meets Heaven—A Pilgrimage* (New York: HarperSanFrancisco, 2007), p. 183.

[17]Ibid., p. 184.

[18]Ibid., p. 185.

[19]M. Therese Lysaught, "Memory, Funerals, and the Communion of Saints: Growing Old and Practices of Remembering," in *Growing Old in Christ,* ed. Stanley Hauerwas, Carole Bailey Stoneking and Keith G. Meador (Grand Rapids: Eerdmans, 2003), p. 285.